Bad Fat
Black Girl

Bad Fat Black Girl

NOTES FROM A
TRAP FEMINIST

Sesali Bowen

AMISTAD

An Imprint of HarperCollinsPublishers

HarperCollins books may be purchased for educational, business, or sales promotional use. For information, please email the Special Markets Department at SPsales@harpercollins.com.

FIRST HARPERCOLLINS PAPERBACK PUBLISHED IN 2022

Designed by Leah Carlson-Stanisic

Library of Congress Cataloging-in-Publication Data is available upon request.

ISBN 978-0-06-311174-5

22 23 24 25 26   LSC   10 9 8 7 6 5 4 3 2 1

For all the real bitches

Contents

TRAP FEMINISM

This for my jazzy bitches, classy bitches,
Oh yeah, my ratchet bitches.

—Yo Gotti, "I Wanna Fuck"[1]

Throughout my entire college career, and for years after, I was the proud owner of a 2007 Pontiac Grand Prix. I named her Sandy because she was the exact same hue as the manufactured beaches off Lake Michigan. A few years later, after the Fetty Wap song dropped, I nicknamed her my "Trap Queen" because for the better part of a decade she'd made sure I made it to classes, to work, to get my hair done, to pick up weed, to rescue home-girls from the homes of shady niggas, to pull off getaways after my homegirls got payback on those same niggas, to countless dick appointments, and into two car accidents. Sandy had heated leather seats and a sound system that allowed everyone to hear me coming from a block away when I had the volume all the way up. Some of the best and worst times of my life happened in the driver's seat (and sometimes the back seat) of that car. You'll hear quite a bit about Sandy later. Her name is probably the only one besides mine that hasn't been changed for this book.

Anyway, I was definitely in Sandy's driver's seat when I heard Memphis rapper Yo Gotti's "I Wanna Fuck" for the first time. I was three years into college at the best public institution in Illinois, without a degree in sight thanks to my struggling GPA. My cousin had recently graduated high school and joined my friends and me in the midwestern cornfields to attend the local community college. She was living without parental supervision for the first time in her life, and it didn't take long for her boyfriend from Chicago to join her in her off-campus apartment. The three of us spent a lot of time together riding around and smoking weed, which probably explains my GPA. It was on one of our many trips that her boyfriend slid his bootleg copy of Yo Gotti's mixtape *Cocaine Muzik 4* into Sandy's CD player. He never got it back.

The disc quickly collected scratches from going in and out of my rotation. I listened to track 4, "I Wanna Fuck," the most because the first verse felt like it had been written for me. I was occasionally jazzy, sometimes classy, but mostly ratchet— just like the women he was shouting out at the top of the verse. And though I've never sucked dick in a club, which was another one of his identifiers of such a lady, there was an incident at the now-closed Lux Lounge in Washington, DC, where a dude put his dick in my hand and I took my precious time removing it. The point is, as a sexually open-minded Black girl, I felt seen by Gotti. This verse was his playful ode to those among us who were willing to put our wigs in a rubber band and let loose during a night out. It's not often, in any genre of music, that women who also looked forward to the . . . after-the-club activities have been celebrated, as opposed to shamed and shitted on for it.

The more I listened to the song, the more attention I paid to the second part of the verse, where Gotti took his affirmation a step further. Right after a particularly childish line where he tried to distance himself from cunnilingus by suggesting that he only ate at Waffle or Huddle House, he laid out one of the most thoughtful, empathetic, responsible, and equitable casual sex scenarios that I'd ever heard in this context. I was grateful for a reference to his favorite condom brand, even if it was the gold-wrapped Magnums that smell like a literal latex factory and make the inside of my vagina feel dry and itchy like a burlap sack. Safe sex is an underrated wave that more people should be on but is often glossed over in music, movies, and TV, where sex is frequently depicted with an undertone of urgency and reckless spontaneity.

Gotti also completely detached himself from the hypocritical, shame-on-you-hoe finger wagging that male privilege emboldens so many Black men to do, especially in hip-hop. In fact, he explicitly stated that he could still respect her after their first-night encounter because, shit, he was there too. At one point in the verse he was almost encouraging her to stand pridefully in her decision and not use intoxication to justify her decision to bust it open for a Memphis nigga. In other words, Gotti didn't devalue or dehumanize this woman because she decided to give him some pussy. He wasn't ashamed, and for that very reason, he didn't think she should be either.

I wish I could say every man I've fucked made me feel the same way. But this verse would do.

To be clear, Yo Gotti didn't write a feminist manifesto. Having followed his career and different interviews he's done, I would argue that he could benefit from a YouTube video or two on Black feminism. If I'm lucky, he'll read this book, but I digress. Gotti *did* lay out an alternative to how women, especially Black women, in similar situations are too often represented: acting only on the sexual desires of men, of lesser moral character for doing so, and not worth the respect of the same men who want to fuck them. I was already hyperaware of this dynamic and actively navigating it in my personal life. However, this verse made me reconsider how women were being talked about in trap music—a hip-hop subgenre that expresses some of the realities and aspirational views of Black folks from the hood—and how those narratives held up against the regular degular women I knew in the real world. From that moment, I felt like I needed to relisten to all the trap music I loved and reconsider what I was being offered.

Despite its mainstream popularity, trap music is still considered one of hip-hop's lowest forms. Part of this stems from elitist assumptions about Southern Black culture, including the accents and unique version of African American vernacular, and respectability politics. However, trap music is also often dismissed because of its representation and treatment of women. As a feminist, I'd often considered the question of why I not only subjected myself to it but also reveled in it. Sitting with Gotti's verse pushed me beyond my frequent cop-out

trap:

Atlanta slang for the specific dwelling or neighborhood where drugs, guns, or other illicit products or services are sold. The term is multifaceted and flexible. When used as a verb, "trapping" means hustling. You can use "trap bitch/nigga," or simply "trapper," to describe someone who hustles, typically in an underground economy. Trap music got its name because its pioneering artists were indeed trap niggas, and the lyrical content reflects the realities of the trap.

response: "Trap music is problematic and sexist, but I like the beats." Like every other staple of Black women's lives, it was more complicated than that.

Still, it felt initially counterintuitive to look for examples of affirming language in trap, a genre that had been labeled aggressively reductive. But there was a reason some trap songs made me put more bass in my voice when I shouted the lyrics over Sandy's speakers, or put my hands in the air at the club. I suddenly paid more attention to all the times Gucci Mane also openly rapped about his partners having abortions. I thought differently about Travis Porter letting a female's voice dominate their single "Make It Rain" with a straightforward demand: "You wanna see some ass, I wanna see some cash."[2] And what about *all* of the female rap I'd been devouring since I was old enough to control the radio?

Female rappers have often echoed the sentiments of male rappers: that sex and desire are indeed transactional. But the formula laid out on Trick Daddy's 1998 single "Nann," when the baddest bitch, Trina, insisted, "You don't know nann hoe done been the places I been, who can spend the grands that I spend, fuck 'bout five or six best friends,"[3] implied that there was also an art to the specific role women played in those interactions. On "Big Ole Freak," Megan Thee Stallion says, "You can't take no nigga from me, I got mind control."[4] That's not the position of a passive receiver of male attention but that of a strategic mastermind set on creating sexual relationships on her own terms. Over decades of listening to female rappers, I learned to prioritize my own desires, ambitions, and pleasures, because for all the ways that they might reflect how men talk about us in their rhymes, these women are also adding a key piece of nuance that these niggas would rather everyone overlook: women, *especially* Black women, are inherently valuable.

This was the beginning of trap feminism for me: the moment I realized I was evolving not away from trap but in a full circle back to it. I wouldn't accept the idea that no good could come out of trap music. I wanted to reconcile the fact that some of my favorite trap songs made me, a queer Black woman, feel good, proud, and even inspired. Perhaps not all of the lyrics about women were cause for outrage or dismissal; actual descriptions of Black girl joy, Black girl genius, and Black girl survival were at play, even if unintentional.

In the past, trap seemed to be at odds with the rest of my identity as a feminist. I'd been advocating for Black women, leading organizing efforts around issues like free access to birth control, and teaching incoming freshmen about rape culture. But now it no longer seemed contradictory to be bumping Gucci or Jeezy at full volume while whipping Sandy around campus. I'd taken a gender studies course with the brilliant Dr. Ruth Nicole Brown about Black girlhood, where we were encouraged to sit with the fullness of being both Black and girl identified. She was one of the first people to put the bug in my ear that what other people saw as chaotic, deviant, or just ghetto as hell was the stuff Black girl fire was made of. My grades finally improved when I changed my major to gender studies, and I learned how to take deeper dives into the media I was consuming. I was listening to trap differently, and I didn't have to justify shaking my ass to Waka Flocka Flame, while still demanding respect as a woman. I didn't know it, but I was formulating the basis for what would become my personal soapbox, my philosophy, and my own dogma: trap feminism.

I said "trap feminism" out loud for the first time during a road trip from Washington, DC, to Chicago. By that time I'd already been writing about pop culture through a feminist lens at Feministing.com. I was calling out Miley Cyrus for cultural appropriation during her weird twerking phase and advocating for more representation of fat girls on-screen. I'd finally seen myself through six years of undergrad (I had to transfer to a completely new university because I'd exhausted all of my financial aid appeals at the university in the cornfields) and had a gender studies degree to show for it. I'd been recognized as a reproductive justice activist. I was a "good" feminist.

Midway through our twelve-hour ride, my homegirl and I exited the highway at a rest stop to grab some Burger King and empty our bladders. Somehow we found ourselves staring at a bulletin board with the faces of missing persons looking back at us. An overwhelming amount of them were Black girls still in their teens. These flimsy pieces of paper likely to be overlooked were probably the strongest effort that would be made from the authorities to bring any of them home. It's one of those hard pills you learn to swallow as a Black girl, and rather than rage against it, you just try your damnedest not to go missing.

Neither my homegirl nor I wondered if any of those Black girls staring back at us had had an unfortunate run-in with a serial killer or were captured to have their organs harvested on the black market. With our Whoppers in hand and bitter resolve in our hearts, we both resigned ourselves to the more familiar, but just as disturbing, possibility: these girls were most likely in the company of Black men and working in the sex trade at their behest. We shared a brief, silent moment filled with recognizable disgust and anger, having been confronted once again with the reality that Black women often face the most intimate forms of violence at the hands of Black men.

Male rappers still sell a fantasy of pimping women who are so enamored by their men's charms that they're willing to seduce and sleep with other men to make the man they've devoted themselves to richer. They sell a version of pimping that ignores the social, economic, and physical risks for women in these relationships, assuming that the kind of women who get into the game are already too far gone. No one takes the time to separate the pimping that rappers talk about from the reality of sex trafficking for most young Black women: getting turned out by grown, manipulative, violent, and lazy ass men who aren't willing to make money by more ethical means, like, in my opinion, sucking dick to earn it themselves.

Back in the car at the rest stop, homegirl and I spent a bunch of time talking about the dissonance of being Black girls in community with Black men but also subject to their sexism, and that of the rest of the world. At some point in the dialogue, probably in between recounting the first time an adult man propositioned me to "get some money from these niggas," which he clearly wanted to pocket for himself, and still loving Lil Wayne's verse on "Where da Cash At," I mentioned my love for Gotti's "I Wanna Fuck" verse. As we danced through words and whatever music Sandy was playing, we laughed and tsked as we easily transitioned from joy to shame to optimism to hopelessness. It was complicated, and that was okay. "This whole conversation is like . . . trap feminism," I suggested. I glanced over at her, waiting for a reaction that would tell me whether or not this was corny. It wasn't. She agreed, and that was my green light to keep going and keep talking.

Eight years later, trap music is already giving way to something else. The hood (the ghetto, the place where poor Black folks hustle and get by the best way they know how with sometimes tragic and sometimes brilliant outcomes) is no longer central to the experiences of artists in the genre. There is an entire new class of rappers who seem to have hopped straight from the depressed, angsty corner of Tumblr and onto Sound-Cloud. They rock rainbow-colored hair and pop antianxiety meds before they party. Some of these lil niggas aren't niggas at all but white boys from obscure parts of America. But no matter what generation or genre of hip-hop we look at, or how much it evolves, men remain at the center. The codes inscribed onto women, gender, and sexuality remain relatively the same. Niggas with face tattoos and low-cut fades, former drug dealers, or even hotep-adjacent niggas like Kendrick Lamar and J. Cole all still describe the same type of bitches in their songs. Women who are thick, but not plus-size, with little waists and big butts. They describe sexual partners who are just as obsessed with their wealth as they are and eager for an opportunity to be in proximity. The women are assumed to be looking to men for a dollar, a come up, the promise of love and loyalty, or all of the above. All of these rappers want access to those women, like accessories, and feel emboldened to dictate the standards they think those women should live by.

If you have invested in those kinds of gender dynamics, it's easy to deduce that trap music, or hip-hop in general, is only meant to speak to and represent men. And so long as this is the case, trap feminism is necessary. Thankfully, I've rarely been the kind of bitch rappers spit about. I'm built differently, physically and mentally. I prioritize Black women in all things, and I'm always going to question the assignments given to me. Being this way has put me in the perfect position to see that trap music is actually rich with nuances we've overlooked, and there's even more sitting right on the periphery.

Female rap was the first frontier for trap feminism, way before I had a name for it. I already mentioned the blueprint Trina set for me. But I was just as enamored by the likes of Foxy Brown, Jackie O, La Chat, and Shawnna. I'm proud to bear witness to the new crop of female rappers blossoming right

hotep:

An Egyptian word that means "at peace." However, it is used colloquially by Black folks to describe people who are aligned with sexism, homophobia, respectability, and a lot of conspiracy theories, all in service of being "pro-Black" or Afrocentric. They often tend to romanticize the continent of Africa, using terribly painted images of pharaohs and other African monarchs to represent their views or identity.

alongside the dudes. Bbymutha has four kids, proudly rocks synthetic wigs as opposed to twelve-hundred-dollar virgin hair bundles, and will tell you so on a track. City Girls, the rap duo who repopularized the word "period," enjoy a reckless disregard for men and the law in their pursuit of cash. Doja Cat is giving Tyler, the Creator a run for his money as an imaginative MC *and* a lusty admirer of white boys. Rico Nasty and Asian Da Brat are musical iterations of Audre Lorde's "The Uses of Anger." Yes, I said it. These are just a few examples in a beautiful range of female rappers envisioning so many different versions of Black girlhood that claps right back. Black women's greatest strength is that we are always more than what everyone says we are, and we've never been afraid to put people on notice about it, both on and off mic. We live lives that are complex, political, and sometimes contradictory.

I know women who've fucked people on the first night and still made it to their corporate jobs or college classes, on time, the next day. The strippers I know are also writers, anime geeks, parents, weed aficionados, cooks, and students. And then there is me: Educated, but always willing to throw these hands. With a head full of foundational feminist texts and theories that helps me question everything I once thought I knew about gender and race. And with a deep love for Gucci Mane, the same rapper known for such gems as "Imma treat her like a dog, feed her like a dog, beat her like a dog, then pass her to my dogs."[5] Fat, and sometimes struggling to find clothes that fit my body, but still feeling like a bad bitch and aspiring to be an ever badder. Fuck what you heard—Black women have never been basic. Whether you believe us or not is up to you.

I developed trap feminism as a framework to understand how Black women have influenced and are influenced by trap culture, a term that deserves a little bit of clarification. I had the opportunity (on the Clubhouse app) to ask producer Mike Will Made It how he felt about trap culture being appropriated and diluted with the spread of the music. He responded with the observation that even the phrase "trap culture" waters down what he understands trapping to be: hustling. I agree with him. Most of the time in this book I'll be using "trap culture" as a way to talk about the economies, language, and ideologies of young people in the hood, not the music industry or the personas of its artists. However, as a media scholar and professional, I can't ignore the ways in which trap music is meant to be reflective of the raw spirit of the trap itself in addition to communicating the sexual, financial, and cultural aspirations of its young people. Trap feminism lives right at this intersection between the reality and the rehearsed, overhearing the conversations between the two and trying to sort through what all of it means, using my own lived experiences as points of reference.

Beyond its purely intellectual endeavors, trap feminism is also a guiding principle in how I live my life—a belief system that informs my specific version of empowerment. Just like the musical genre and the broader culture it represents, my trap feminism isn't perfect. It's not diplomatic or polished. It's not organized or even decipherable to everyone. But it works to describe a certain kind of ethos that serves Black girls who grew up physically fighting for the shit we believe in, those of us who aren't afraid to say "Fuck these niggas" and ride for our homegirls just as hard as we've been taught to ride for men. Trap feminism says that Black girls who have ever rocked bamboo earrings, dookie braids, Baby Phat, lace fronts, or those who have worked as hoes, scammers, call-center reps, at day cares, in retail, and those who sell waist trainers and mink lashes on Instagram are all worth the same dignity and respect we give Michelle Obama and Beyoncé. In the face of anti-Black sexism, racism, and capitalism, we navigate our creative expression, our sexual desires, and our difficult decisions every day without a framework. But we *deserve* a framework, and we actually need it the most.

If you want to break it down into academic jargon, here's how I wrote about it in a college essay: "Trap feminism acknowledges the ways in which Black girls might benefit from and enjoy performing racialized gender in ways that have been deemed inappropriate, reductive, and unproductive." For example, white folks, and even some bougie Black folks, think that Black women wearing bonnets outside the house is ghetto, tacky, and classless. However, not only do we face consequences for having hair that is seen as disruptive, unkempt, or unprofessional, but also getting our hair done often costs money and time. In order to maximize that investment, Black women use items like bonnets to preserve our hairdos for the moments

dookie braids:

Jumbo box braids.

lace fronts:

Lace-front wigs are those where either human or synthetic hair has been tied to delicate, sheer lace by hand. This allows the wearer to have a natural, custom hairline. They were once reserved for actors and other performers, but Black women and queer folks are pioneering new ways to style and wear them daily.

when they need to look their best. Or we're covering unkempt hair while in between hairdos. It's a strategic decision that allows us to manage our personal upkeep on our own terms. This is just one example of Black-girl expression that gets shitted on, but there are so many more.

These are the kinds of performances and expressions of Black femininity—our style, our language, our expressions, etc.—that are often mined, extracted, and appropriated by outside communities and institutions but still read as useless when enacted by Black women. I've found that we engage some of these modes of expression, like twerking, just for fun. But others, like making sure our hair lasts for two weeks at work so that we're not accused of looking incompetent, are actually methods of survival and creativity. Trap feminism is often hiding in plain sight: at a Hot Girl Summer pool party, in your nigga's DMs, or in line at the public-assistance office.

In the time since that road trip when I first uttered the phrase "trap feminism" to my friend, I've added another gender studies degree to my credentials. I wrote a thesis on Black girls and memes and called it "Bitches Be Like . . ." I've covered hip-hop, especially its female players, for the past few years as an entertainment editor for several major women's publications. This book builds off that expertise. It rests on the shoulders, and is in some ways an update, of Joan Morgan's 1999 hip-hop feminist text *When Chickenheads Come Home to Roost.* My love for trap makes me what Roxane Gay would call a "bad feminist."

Dr. Ruth Nicole Brown made space for me to celebrate Black girlhood in this specific way.

I can articulate trap feminism because I've read feminist theory and explored the entertainment industry in my career, but that's not why I understand it at such a cellular level. Before I had a name for it, and before I realized female rappers were so often talking directly to me, trap feminism was written into the codes I learned growing up broke, curious, Black, resilient, and female in some of the worst parts of Chicago. It's what I learned through fistfights, sex work, queerness, and fatness. It was part of a tool kit I used to survive, thrive, and be able to tell somebody else about it. It's still how I navigate and make sense of the world.

That's why this book isn't *just* an analysis of trap music or *just* a straightforward feminist textbook. It's also a retelling of those formative experiences. A lot of my life is filled with what other people see as only ratchet chaos, trifling debauchery, and that strong dissonance my homegirl and I were trying to break down on a road trip with Sandy. It's a look back at the lessons I'm glad I've learned, the ones I wish I'd never had to, and how I'm a more solid bitch because I did. This is not a self-help book, but it is about how I built confidence and figured out self-love in the face of a rhetoric that said I shouldn't. There were days when self-preservation was all I had, and on other days I found myself transcending boundaries and sometimes my wildest dreams. Trap feminism makes sense of all of it.

Even though these stories are mine, I'm not alone in them. I know girls like me, I grew up with girls like me, and I've lived a lot of what you'll read here with girls like me by my side. Today, I'm perhaps most aware of all the girls like me I've never met and never will meet. None of us needs validation from anyone else but ourselves, and by the time you finish this book, you hopefully won't be tempted to question the perceived self-assurance of the next Black girl you meet. But while we don't require acknowledgment, we deserve to be seen. It's time for us to be our own master teachers and name our experiences for what they are, as we live them. I've been paying attention to these details for a while now, and lucky for you, I took some notes.

Chapter 1

BAD BITCHES ONLY

Why this bitch keep hittin' my line?
She knowin' she ain't no dime and shit.

—Gucci Mane, "Pussy Print"[1]

I'm fat. Let's start there. Not only am I fat, the ancestors saw fit to deny me the proportions that are so frequently admired in other Black women. Rather than collect my excess in rounded hips and ass, most of it has decided to settle in my arms, back, and what I affectionately call my tire: the circumference around my lower abdomen, which includes the space above where my ass crack ends and my sagging belly. "Flat" is an understatement when describing my ass. My butt is more square shaped than anything else, and from certain angles it appears to be actively trying to squeeze itself into the rest of me, perhaps hoping even after all of these years to get some of the jiggle the rest of my body has in abundance. I'm tall—not WNBA tall, but at five foot eight, I'm taller than most women—and my legs didn't seem to get the memo about what size the rest of my body wanted to be. If I'm a size 22 up top, I'm a size 18 in the legs. For the sake of comparison, it was once said on Facebook that I'm shaped not unlike a wisdom tooth. On my more disparaging days I feel boxy. When I'm feeling more gracious and accepting, which is the majority of the time, I settle on "wavy" as a good descriptor of what I look like. It's more than curvy but soft and jiggly. According to the kids (by "kids," I mean folks of all ages who body-shame on the internet), I'm "built bad."

I've always been fat. I didn't get pregnant or have a medical condition that caused me to gain weight. My metabolism didn't slow down as I got older, causing my weight to suddenly skyrocket. I was called Buddha Baby when I was an infant because I was so round and damn near bald. There's a picture of me sitting on top of one of my granddaddy's Cadillacs, not even a year old yet, with the strap of my summer onesie falling off one shoulder and exposing a whole infant boob. In fourth grade, I wore a stretchy knit dress that touched my ankles along with my first pair of chunky, platform heels (if two and a half inches count as heels). I felt sexy and cool, like the sixth Spice Girl. Seeing me in the getup, my granny couldn't contain her laughter or her assessment that I actually looked like "a stuffed sausage." My body has always been in excess of what is deemed acceptable and appropriate, and outside what we're told is sexy and pretty. In elementary, middle, and high schools I was one of the fat kids. It was a sin made worse as I aged, and instead of acclimating, I just became more wavy. I have been reminded of this failure often and loudly.

There is a myth that Black people aren't fat phobic—and bigger Black women, by extension, are confident and unaffected by their size—and we need to put that to rest right now. Generally speaking, Black people do have a higher tolerance for body fat on feminine bodies than other groups do. We like our women to have "some meat on their bones," "something to grab on to," or to put it plainly, we like them "thick." But thick and fat are not the same thing. The difference between being a "big fine" and just being "big" has as much, if not more, to do with body shape as it does with body mass. A woman twice my weight can still be stamped "bad bitch" if she carries her weight everywhere but her midsection. Hourglass and pear-shaped women are typically celebrated amongst Black folks and idolized in trap music. Young Dolph said, "If she ain't got a fat ass, then she can't get up in this car."[2] Describing a girl he shouldn't have to fuck "for free," Drake said her "stomach on flat flat . . . ass on what's that."[3] I could go on for days, but you get where I'm heading here. There is a formula for what makes a bad bitch, and it starts with an impressive hip-to-waist ratio. Right beyond that, though, are the familiar trappings of fat phobia.

You ever peep how many exceptions to the hourglass standard are made for Black girls who are thinner? Think: Rihanna, Ciara, Halle Berry, Tyra Banks, or any of the unshapely, skinny light-skinned girls you went to school with. We call those women who are shaped less like hourglasses and more like the hour hand on a clock "slim thick" or "model material" and keep it moving without comment. Have you ever noticed that there are no such concessions made for fat Black girls, ever? White beauty norms will always find themselves a seat at the table, even ours,

bad bitch:

A woman/femme who impresses herself and others by way of her body, success, attitude, style, fashion, values, and/or behavior.

and that includes vicious fat phobia. If you're a Black girl like me, with the misfortune of being both fat and "built bad," existing outside the aesthetic rules means that you've committed an egregious act against the social order. Women who find themselves too far away from the center of beauty norms are often treated as if they've committed treason, our aesthetic a public-facing betrayal of our refusal to conform, our refusal to go to any lengths necessary to be valuable to society—specifically, to its men.

Beauty is a politicized concept precisely because it maintains what bell hooks calls "imperialist, capitalist, white supremacist patriarchy,"[4] a system of oppression that gives all of us something to aspire to. As such, sexism simultaneously serves the interests of men *and* capitalism by assigning value to only those women who are read as beautiful by cultural gatekeepers. It creates a culture in which women are taught to lead with their bodies, to remain open to their bodies being judged at any moment and all moments, and to internalize those judgments as commentary on their place within the culture. Rewarding and praising women who meet these standards, while shaming or erasing those who don't, in turn, reinforces the masculinity and heterosexuality of the men around them because the presumed desires of men are the litmus test. In order to formalize and institutionalize this process, feminine beauty has become an actual form of capital and currency that everyone gets to leverage, directly or indirectly, depending on their level of privilege. The thing about any ethos is that much of it relies on some "mythmaking": a top-line, fantasy version of events has to exist in order to set the standard for everyone else to aspire to. This narrative is typically what serves white supremacist capitalist sexism the best. It's the center of a wheel, and those closest to that center benefit the most from it, creating an optic of exclusivity and inaccessibility that helps keep those on the margins the most disenfranchised, despite the fact that we do so much work to keep the shit spinning.

Trap culture is heavily invested in the ethos of bad bitches only. Here achieving feminine beauty comes with the promise of access to wealth, love, happiness, and autonomy. A bad bitch on a nigga's arm, then, is meant to send a message about his financial and social status, his style, and even his manhood. This is part of the reason why girls like Lira Galore, Miracle Watts, Bria Myles, and Alexis Skyy—all of them with fat asses, flat stomachs, and millions of followers on Instagram—become celebrities in their own right. They represent an explicitly feminine version of a Black American dream that puts them in league with the rich and powerful just because of the presumed influence that accompanies their serpentine frames.

Bad bitches are supposed to make niggas move differently in their pursuit of them. They are the exceptional creatures who can temporarily pull niggas away from their more pressing matters, like making money and supporting their friends and family. Bad bitches are their hobby, a recreational activity that comes with the territory of being coined up and widely respected. In almost every version of the trap ethos, niggas open their wallets and dole out gifts in the form of big Chanel bags for bad bitches to carry around in all different colors; brand-new Range Rovers for bad bitches to drive to spas and Gucci stores; designer clothes and expensive lace-front wigs for bad bitches to wear; diamond jewelry that makes bad bitches look more expensive; and cosmetic surgery procedures that make bad bitches even badder. If she's both a bad bitch and conveniently loyal to him, he may even soften a little bit emotionally. In these cases, bad bitches get the love and loyalty of men who have been socialized not to give either. But there is no happily ever after, or even once upon a time, without a body that serves this narrative.

So what happens to women like me, who upon first glance aren't what most people would call a bad bitch? According to the ethos, women who don't live up to the feminine ideal—your basic bitches, your ugly bitches, and especially your fat bitches—signify struggle, poverty, poor taste, and lesser value. In any version of the story, they don't exist or have any access to men who can provide the blessings that bad bitches get. I'll never forget how this rhetoric showed up when Usher, the veteran R&B singer I've loved since I was a little girl and an artist who has committed to maintaining trap-music influences in his music, was involved in a sex scandal in 2017. Court documents were leaked that revealed he'd settled a lawsuit for over a million dollars with a woman who accused him of exposing her to genital herpes. After the news went public, more women lawyered up and came forward with their own accusations against the singer, and one of them was a fat woman named Quantasia Sharpton.

When women come forward about being wronged in any capacity by men they've slept with, especially men who are rich and powerful, the general public rarely rushes to their defense. When it comes to these kinds of men, the ones who hold the keys to millions of hearts and millions of dollars, women who find themselves in their company are expected to be happy about it. I expected some distrust toward anyone who said they'd had regrets about fucking the dude who made "Nice & Slow," but it was different for Quantasia. I scrolled in horror as Twitter and Instagram had a field day with memes and jokes based on the perception that her body was proof of a lie, because someone like Usher would never fuck her. As the story continued to play out in the media, representatives for Usher's team reached out to *TMZ* to officially deny the accusations by echoing the sentiment that my good sis was not his type. His previously demonstrated taste in women, and not his medical records, were meant to put the whole matter to rest.

This dissonance was familiar to me. As a fat girl in middle school and high school, many of my interactions with boys were soiled by these body politics. Most boys in my peer group wouldn't be caught dead giving me a compliment. Some of them would make fun of each other by suggesting the other one was attracted to me. I'd walk down a hallway, or past a group of them on the street, and one of them would say to the other, "That's you right there." I'd hold my breath for the inevitable laughter from the others. Because not enough boys are taught how to value women they don't find attractive, even the possibility of friendship was aggressively rejected by boys still trying to put together their own fragile masculine identities.

When I was a high school sophomore, I went on a multi-city HBCU tour with about two dozen other students. One of them was a male upperclassman I'll call Rob. Rob was one of those guys who was lame precisely because he so desperately wanted to be cool. He was a little husky but not bad looking. He followed the fashion trends set by Chicago teens in the early aughts: a rotation of sneakers that matched his oversize jerseys and T-shirts. But as a wise man once said, you can't buy swag.

For all Rob's color coordination, he was still a fucking cornball. But on this off-campus trip, where he was not only one of the oldest students but also one of the only dudes among us, he was feeling himself. I suspect that the freedom of being away from home, and his peers who all liked somebody else more than him, combined with the promise of under-supervised overnights, had him feeling like he needed to make his desires, and non-desires, known. Despite all of my attempts at friendliness, I could feel an intensified coldness coming from him as we traveled the South by bus. He spent the entire trip picking fights with me, cutting me off during conversations, making fun of me, and trying to embarrass me whenever we ended up grouped together. My breaking point came when he flat-out told me to "shut the fuck up" during an impromptu gathering in one of the hotel rooms. Full stop. "No, you shut *your* bitch ass up!" I spat back, trying to match his venomous energy. His subtle shots had transitioned into outright disrespect, and it was only because our chaperones heard the commotion and came in to physically restrain me that I didn't lay hands on him. As the adults tried to piece together how such animosity had escalated between us, seemingly out of nowhere, a female upperclassman laid it out for them. "He thinks Sesali likes him and he keeps trying to intimidate her."

Rob was calmer after that, as if his cover had been blown. He had been punishing me for daring to exist in his orbit, let alone anticipate that he'd engage in niceties. For the record, he was a lame and I wasn't attracted to him, but I still felt that blow of rejection, even if I hadn't applied for it. I also learned a valuable lesson from the female classmate's welcomed revelation. It was one of my earliest lessons that how people treat me and respond to my body sometimes has very little to do with me and everything to do with them and their own identities.

Creating visible distance between themselves and me, I began to understand, was just one of the ways in which boys and men policed their own immature version of straight masculinity. They made sure they were being the right kind of boys by being outwardly attracted to the right kind of girls. Those girls who were usually some combination of lighter and smaller than me. Boys did their own checks and balances at my expense, and like most teenage girls, I began to internalize the idea that the approval of men was of the utmost importance. I learned to shut down my own desires and refused to proactively move on my own romantic interests first, because I needed a green light and some form of positive affirmation. Make no mistake: I've never been meek or timid in the presence of men, whether or not I had crushes on them. I would threaten, fight, or roast the fuck out of boys who went out of their way to hurt my feelings in public. Disrespect is disrespect and not tolerated in this household. But at home with my journal and my thoughts, the rejection felt like knives piercing my spirit, because it didn't feel circumstantial. It felt like a permanent, recurring part of my life as a fat girl. I was always relatively popular and fit in, but I still saw my body as a kind of failure that brought me nothing but shame, humiliation, and disappointment.

This was true even though I warranted sexual attention from some of those same boys, and other men, when we were alone. Averted stares, awkward silences, and chuckles in school hallways, where the watchful eyes of our peers were the dominating forces, suddenly turned into shouts from car windows, summonings in the form of "Aye, lil mama," and light grabs at my wrists as I walked home from the bus stop or the corner store by myself. It was still rare that I experienced the same softening I witnessed between men and the girls they thought were worthy of walking arm-in-arm with, though. Being a big girl often meant they couldn't risk an emotional attachment that could become permanent or public. It was another reminder that I was not one of the bad bitches. I was too big to be worthy of their rare displays of chivalry and valiance.

One day, when I was in my late teens or early twenties, I

made a slick comment to one of the dudes in my aunt's apartment complex about him eating my pussy. It was a crass joke loaded with the same energy men use when they tell others to suck their dicks—a playful "Fuck you," if you will. I laughed it off with my cousin and went on about my day. This guy wasn't my friend, but I knew him. The apartment complex was small, and if you were one of the young-adult residents, you spent a lot of time outside. I hadn't thought that I was flirting with him, and we'd never exchanged that kind of energy, but clearly my remark had planted some kind of seed in his head. Later that night, I didn't even hear him come into my cousin's bedroom, where I was sleeping alone.

With my eyes still closed, I felt someone touching me in a clear attempt to wake me up. Assuming it was one of my cousins, or a friend playing around, I waved him off and tried to roll out of reach to get back to sleep. "It's me," he whispered, followed by his name. He said it confidently, as if my familiarity with his name would negate the creepy inappropriateness of him suddenly standing over me, uninvited, in a home that belonged to neither of us. As I regained a full awareness of my surroundings and the reality of what was happening sunk in, I waved him off again, this time with a firm, "Uhn-uh." Normally my cousin would have been sleeping beside me, but she wasn't there on this night. I'd never wanted to hear her snores more.

I knew what he wanted, and I wasn't interested. I'd hoped that by limiting my movements and making it clear that sleep was more important to me than the dick he was offering, he'd drop the whole thing and leave. He didn't. He kept groping me, at one point grabbing my head and trying to push my face toward his crotch. This jolted me fully awake, and I sat up disgusted. He took that as a cue to go even further and began grabbing at my hips. I tried to silently evade him out of fear that my aunt would wake up, see this nigga in her crib, and think I'd invited him in. I was also scared to find out just how persistent he would be in his pursuit. I'd started to mentally resign myself to what was going to happen, opting out of causing a scene. In a low voice that sounded more annoyed than anything else, I looked him in the eye and said, "If you're going to rape me, can you at least use a condom?"

That's when he stopped. He said something along the lines of "What!? You trippin'." And then he scoffed. This muthafucka had the audacity to scoff *at me*. Mentioning the word "rape" had startled and offended him. It was clear to me at that moment he hadn't even considered the possibility that he was violating me. For him, that was just how you were supposed to fuck fat girls: in the dead of night, when the fewest amount of people could see you, without the slightest pretense of romance, after expressing absolutely zero desire toward her before the moment you wanted your dick inside her, even if you have to wake her up out of a deep sleep to do it, and whether she wants to or not. By calling it rape, *I* was the one being irrational and killing the vibe. I should have been okay with what was happening.

To keep it real with you, there have been instances when I *was* okay with this kind of treatment. I've agreed to fuck with shady niggas on their terms and not mine because I believed for a long time that I deserved whatever treatment I got. After all, I wasn't a bad bitch. Perhaps that's why, when I look back on that situation, it's not the sexual assault that hurts the most. Word of what happened got around (because that's what happens in small apartment complexes where people are outside all the time). My cousin got it back to me that no one believed that I had been truly wronged, or that I had had very little control in the situation, or that I could have possibly been in danger, because: "Look how big she is." To this day, that is what stings the most and what I'll never forget. My body made it harder for even my own community to be empathetic, protective, or compassionate toward me, something I already knew about the rest of the world.

I've been ridiculed and made fun of just for walking into a roomful of men, as if my mere presence was an affront to their identity and sense of self. Being called "Big Sexy" by men who fix my car or install my internet has been a weird but regular occurrence in my life. It's meant to read as a compliment, but it's actually more of the same checks and balances. It's not a declaration of their attraction to me. It's a declaration that they're going against the grain by not marking me *un*attractive like they're supposed to. I'm a *big* kind of sexy, and there is a difference.

Even interactions that aren't sexually or romantically charged also become opportunities to remind me of the perceived failure of my body. Accidentally bumping into someone on the street has ended with me being reprimanded, not for being careless or clumsy but for having a body that takes up so much space in the first place. A bar manager accepting my bartending application refused to even move forward with the interview. He blatantly told me, "I don't think you can clear the bar. It's tight back here." A man on a flight who was upset that my thighs prevented his full manspreading loudly accosted me for not purchasing two seats. Don't even get me started on being a fat girl on the internet. It's a cesspool of body policing where people regurgitate the body hierarchy over and over again while using it as a license to say whatever the fuck they want about my body at any time. If I leave a public comment that someone doesn't like, or if a stranger just stumbles across a photo of me, it can easily become open season on my waviness. It is the internet that reminds me most often that I am "built bad."

If you do an image search for "fat Black girl" on Google, there is a picture of me on the first page. It's an iPhone photo that my homegirl took of me in Atlanta. I'm wearing a dress that is black up top with a print on the bottom. I have on a grey ombre wig, nonprescription cat-eyed glasses, and Timberland boots. The dress is tight enough that you can see the indentation where my stomach can't decide if it wants to be a single or double entity, and because I'm standing at an angle, you can see my "tire" wrapping its way around my backside. I used this picture as the header image for an article I wrote in 2015 about how white women were dominating the fat acceptance movement, which has made it an accidental SEO success for that specific search phrase. It has also been a hit for internet trolls who use this picture—a picture of me—to make memes about fat women.

The first one I saw placed the photo next to a picture of another woman who was light skinned and very thick, with a small waist, wide hips, and big boobs. It was captioned: "The BBWs I like vs. the BBWs that like me." The implication was that she was a sexy "Big Beautiful Woman" and I was not. The next meme I saw was in a viral Twitter thread that some dude made about the types of chicks you meet in college. He used my picture as an example of a fat chick who thinks she's cute but just dresses well. It was cosigned by hundreds of comments, a few of them by people who wanted to make it clear that they didn't like my body or my outfit. Then, on a Facebook post, a woman used my picture to talk about how women with my body type weren't wife material or worthy of any prioritization because they don't take care of their bodies. She took it down when I privately messaged her. Hearing directly from my own mouth that the post was hurtful and damaging had affected her. Apparently, she realized that fat Black girls were humans and not just unsavory ideas. In the face of this kind of bullshit, I still intentionally go by BadFatBlackGirl on social media. It's how I remind people that I'm not ashamed of my body, that I still see myself as a bad bitch, and that at the end of the day I'm still just a human Black girl.

Despite the barrage of messages that have suggested I am unlovable, unfuckable, and even unlikable, I have been the recipient of all of the above. I've seen men correct themselves in public after someone caught them checking me out. I'm called "confident" by people of all genders when they can't muster up the courage to call me beautiful against their internalized belief that fatness can't be attractive. There has been no shortage of people, across the gender spectrum, who have been attracted to me. I've been in many different kinds of relationships, and I've had even more kinds of sex. If I'm really doomed to loneliness and invisibility because I'm "built bad," I can't tell.

Unfortunately, size also hasn't stopped some of the other human Black girls I know personally—friends, coworkers, family, mentees, who have all been a source of safety and solace in nearly every other aspect of my life—from being fat phobic. They've berated and judged other women for being fat, as if their words aren't bullets that do damage to anyone in the line of fire, including me. My own dissonance comes in the form of women who claim to admire my confidence but will still let "her fat ass" slip from their tongues, dipped in venom, and shoot past me to someone else. My complicated reality is that I have friends who aren't afraid to look me dead in the eye and complain that they look "fat" in pictures, and I belong to a family of fat women who, for the most part, hate their bodies. I'm the only member of my family, and often the only member of my crew, who has adopted a stance of fat acceptance or fat positivity.

My community of women has taught me a lot about what it means to be independent, resilient, and ambitious. But a way to resist body shaming was not one of those lessons. Even female rappers, whom I also consider a part of my community thanks to all of the life lessons they've imparted through their music, haven't offered me much in the body-image department. One is hard-pressed to even hear a woman mentioned in trap music if she's not a bad bitch by the physical standards, and the female MCs I love have had to find a voice and an identity in an industry that demands that specific presentation.

Most of the women in hip-hop I grew up listening to basked in the glow of having bodies that fit the mold. Trina was the baddest bitch because she's always had a fat ass. Foxy Brown knew that she was model material with her long legs and smooth skin. Even now, City Girls brag about their small-framed bodies, and Megan Thee Stallion knows that niggas are "in love with this ass."[5] Queen Latifah and Missy Elliott played with masculine and androgynous energy rather than commit to the vixen mold. Mia X, La Chat, and Gangsta Boo all talked good shit in their primes, but none of it was clapbacks to people who may have something negative to say about how they looked. These women have taught me how to be confident; they taught me how to finesse; they taught me to deprioritize men; they helped inform the entire theory of trap feminism. But these women were able to execute all of this because they had bodies that gave them the access, a platform, and the attention of people willing to listen.

I can't say I blame my family or friends for spending so much time obsessed with bodies that none of them have, and probably never will. I've done the same. Some of them are struggling to get closer to that center, embarking on journeys toward an ideal that doesn't look like me. Fat phobia is insidious like that. There are very few places to hide from it. It touches all of our lives in some fashion, so when you have a marginalized body sometimes it really do be your own niggas hating the hardest. Nor do I fault women who have hourglass shapes and fill out Fashion Nova dresses the way they're advertised on Instagram, or who revel in the privileges that come with them. All of us are making a way for ourselves under the same ethos. The first time I interviewed Megan Thee Stallion she complained, after we'd wrapped our formal interview, that she didn't have enough hips to match her ass. We've all been touched by the idea that our bodies, if they're built right, are our salvation, our first line of defense, our key to entry. We are all hyperaware that we could always be closer to the center. The material benefits are great, and as I've shown you, the negative outcomes are too ugly.

The bitter truth is that Black women do not have the luxury of resisting the patriarchy by refusing to participate in its beauty mandates. For those of us who are most marginalized, beauty actually becomes a tool that can be used to defend ourselves against racism, sexism, transphobia, classism, etc. We use it to lessen the impact of how we may be otherwise treated for being poor, trans, queer, female, or any other characteristic that the white supremacist capitalist patriarchy subjugates. Black girls get suspended from school and fired from jobs for not having the right hair or the right bodies. Black women who are trans get killed for not fitting cisnormative versions

How to Maintain Your Silk Press, aka Your Wrap

1. Apply an oil sheen or other lightweight moisturizer in order to create a slight hold.

2. Choose any starting point and comb or brush your hair in one direction, so that it eventually "wraps" around the circumference of your head.

3. Use hairpins to keep your hair in place, if necessary, but beware of indentation marks.

4. Once your hair is smoothly wrapped, tie it down with a scarf until you're ready to let your tresses fly free once more.

of beauty. Being bad bitches determines whether we're treated like customers or like criminals when we walk into stores, renters or troublemakers when we try to rent apartments, ladies or targets when we interact with men.

I learned quickly how to stack the bonus points that women earn from adorning themselves in the right way and drawing attention away from what other people could possibly read as our bodies' failures. A fat ass and a small waist can help you skip the line into Club Baddie, but there are definitely other ways to RSVP if you have neither. Growing up in Chicago, a bouncy, layered wrap (basically a blowout named for the daily ritual required to maintain it) made you look refined and elegant, even if you were wearing a Baby Phat puffer below it. It signified to the rest of the world that you could afford to spend a few discretionary dollars on your hair and that you could pull off a classy vibe. So some of the money I made in retail went to getting my hair blow-dried to perfection.

Today, the equivalent is a fresh sew-in or a lace-front wig laid so good that the baby hairs really do appear to be growing from your scalp. Acrylic tips are enjoying a moment of cultural gentrification and heightened popularity, but they've always been the pinnacle of accessorizing for Black femmes. It's literally been years since I haven't had long, painted nails, and I feel like I'm missing a finger when one of them breaks. Clothing choices have always had the power to label you either bad bitch or bum bitch, a hot girl or a hot mess. The first time I had a matching Tommy Hilfiger miniskirt and T-shirt in eighth grade, I thought I'd defeated fat phobia once and for all using the power of a name brand. I have the same feeling today when I'm carrying one of my designer bags and I see the faces of sales associates become more inviting at stores where I might have normally been followed around.

Women level up from just looking good to "being a good look," meaning they look good enough to be the prized bad bitch in the trap fairy tale, when they decorate themselves in the right ways. And while all of this may sound like the maintenance habits of an elite group of Black women with large discretionary budgets, real bitches know you can finesse a lot of this at your local beauty-supply store. Leveraging different privileged aesthetics—lighter skin, decadent accessories and styling, makeup, financial status, etc.—is both a form of resistance and a creative export straight from Black femmes.

More invasive and permanent options to enhance, polish, or completely change the way we look have also become common. There are a bunch of waist trainers, tummy-flattening teas, and plastic surgeons that have become pop-culture icons because they can snatch your waist where Mother Nature did not. And I support girls who choose to take advantage of these options if they can afford to do so safely. As a kid, I used to think that plastic surgery was exclusively for celebrities and rich white people. I was well into adulthood before I personally knew a Black woman who'd had a cosmetic procedure done. Now plastic surgeons are actual celebrities, especially the ones who help

Black women look more like IG models. Dr. Michael Salzhauer, also known as Dr. Miami, went from Snapchatting his surgeries to having his own television series. He even started his own record label after rappers kept asking that their music be featured in his social media videos. Rappers like Plies are casually offering to pay for plastic surgery like it's dinner at Benihana. "Told her if the head fire, swear I'll buy her a new ass,"[6] he spit. I haven't had any work done (yet), but it's honestly kind of refreshing to exist in a time when there are entire online communities who have had or plan to receive Brazilian butt lifts, especially after spending so much of my childhood praying to be shaped less like a wisdom tooth or a stuffed sausage.

I find myself having to defend this pro modification position for two reasons. For one, we've placed a weird morality on bodies that are "natural" and celebrate them over those that have had a little help. The push to "make bodies natural again" is reactive in the face of so many women who've been able to purchase their curves, and it's a huge contradiction. We're inundated with messages that we should be aspiring to be thick and stacked, and we bought a dream that a body marked desirable and built the "right" way is always just around the corner. But women who have the time or resources to pursue those options—and take advantage of the benefits that come from obtaining them—are judged for it. This investment is considered vain, shallow, and self-centered, while spending hours in the gym and extreme dieting are not. At the heart of this contradiction is this: white supremacist capitalist sexism isn't invested just in how women look but in how they relate to their own beauty.

Which brings me to the other reason I have to defend my support of plastic surgery and other enhancements. People think that wanting to change any part of your body means you lack confidence and don't love yourself. They view surgical enhancements as the antithesis of a body positivity that requires you to constantly love your body the way it is, no matter what. This fantasy narrative of body positivity is convenient for people who have no intention of checking their own fat phobia or body-shaming behaviors. I'm expected to love myself no matter what kind of fucked-up shit is said or done to me. This kind of individualistic, introspective body positivity excuses people from being accountable for how they treat marginalized bodies. Nor does it leave room to challenge the limitations of current body standards. I want no part of a fake ass body positivity that allows people to uphold unrealistic standards, shame women for not meeting them, but still demand that we love and embrace our bodies, lest we fall into peer-pressured vanity.

I mentioned the inaccessibility that upholds standards around beauty: only certain people are meant to have access to it, and those few who do should be humble and demure about it. We love that women have fat asses, but we hate when they wear thongs or shake their asses directly into cameras for everyone to see. Women shouldn't know and harness the power of their beauty; they should passively allow the privileges to be bestowed upon them by others. Plastic surgery, or even wearing butt pads, not only threatens the exclusivity of beauty but also *grants women too much control over their beauty.* Issues of access not included, when you can go buy a snatched waist and a fat ass, it democratizes the benefits of having a nice body, which was never how a sexist system was meant to work.

Still, Black girls have found ways to flourish despite these convoluted principles. Multiple studies have concluded that Black women and girls have higher rates of self-esteem and confidence than other female groups. Despite an acute awareness of the extremely narrow beauty standards affecting my life, I also bore witness to women flourishing outside these confines all the time. I knew dark-skinned girls who were cheerleaders at the top of social hierarchies. The best-dressed girl at my high school during freshman year was a light-skinned upperclassman who was plus-size and knew how to contour her face before I knew what contouring was, and she had an older college boyfriend. When I was in college, my same homegirls who had been called weird as preteens for opting out of name-brand jeans to instead experiment with more artsy vibes were suddenly considered mysterious and sexy, like local versions of Janelle Monáe. We all spoke trap's language, proudly, and we were all writing ourselves into the narrative.

Even within the rap game itself, we have more examples than ever of women existing outside that model. Bbymutha, from Tennessee, embraces her self-described saggy titties. Kamaiyah

reps the Bay Area and refuses to play into the male gaze by opting for a West Coast B-girl aesthetic, as opposed to a Kardashian
carbon copy. CupcakKe has built a cult following by combining
raunchy lyrics with a plus-size body and Chicago-hood bitch
energy. Tokyo Vanity has mastered the Instagram–rap–reality
television circuit with a thick New Orleans accent, colorful
weaves, and a big body. Then there's the plus-size phenom
known as Lizzo. Her pop success has allowed her to dominate
the mainstream music industry and still serve bad-bitch realness. The mold has been broken, but only those of us who never
fit it in the first place know it. I firmly believe that being further away from the center gives us the best view. Our vantage
point allows us to see the alternatives, and the cheat codes. In
the space left empty by most of the women in my life, I've developed a body-positive lens that makes room for different kinds of
bodies, no matter how they look or how their owners feel about
them.

I've extended the same kind of openness to women that trap
has extended to its men. For real. If there is any evidence that
the trap can make room for a better body politic, just look at
the niggas who make up most of its musical landscape and
help reestablish its ethos. In Hollywood and fashion, there *are*
beauty standards for men, albeit looser ones. Lighter skin, a
strong jawline, and a dazzling smile can go a long way for men
in these industries. Nice hair, tallness, and broad shoulders
also help. Chiseled biceps and a six-pack are lusty bonuses.
These trap niggas, though? They get to come as they are. The

men who become superstars in this space are just as fat, Black, and stereotypically undesirable as me.

For those maintaining trap's body image ethos, "bad bitch" is an elitist title reserved for only the chosen few, which means the rest of us—the majority—all share a similar lack. By focusing only on women they'd like to fuck, rappers often erase the other Black women who play more pivotal roles in their lives. Their mothers, managers, stylists, fans, baby mamas, childhood friends, publicists, and grandmothers rarely look like the prototype. Not every woman is built like she was destined to work at Magic City. In fact, very few women are built like that, which is why liposuction and BBLs are so common in the first place. On the rare occasion that artists wax poetic about the women who have held them down outside a sexual context, they're usually talking about women who appear across the entire spectrum of body type and size. So when a troll once hopped into my Instagram comments to say I was "built like four grandmas put together" I had a response on deck. "I know. Niggas LOVE they grandmas."

Today, I'm only in conflict with my body when it's time to try on clothes. Other than that, the biggest struggle is trying to uphold the way I see myself against the way the rest of the world does. When I'm naked in front of a mirror, I'm at peace with what I see. I thank the gene god for my good eyebrows and clear skin. My body and its waves are soft and fluffy, like a down comforter. That tire I was talking about earlier does this thing where the top of it sometimes gives off the illusion of a decent hip-to-waist ratio from the front. I wish my legs were longer, but I love the way they're shaped, with meaty thighs tapering off into strong, shapely calves. They rub close together to give me the warm "fat bitch pussy" that Cardi B is obsessed with. My titties don't do anything that a good push-up bra can't remedy. In general, my size has made it so that when I walk into a room, people notice. My very presence in a room often makes people confront their preconceived notions about fat people and who gets to be beautiful.

Which is part of the reason why I had to write this chapter first. There are undoubtedly going to be folks who see what I look like and make assumptions about trap feminism. They are going to question my authority to speak on what trap means to women because I did not first present them with a nice body to look at. Over the course of my career, I've interviewed dozens of women in and around the hip-hop industry and met dozens more. They've been rappers, lawyers, publicists, executives, and CEOs. I can probably count on one hand how many of them were fat. That's not a coincidence. It's because the music industry upholds an unspoken mandate that to take up space in trap as a woman, you must first and foremost look the part. I'm not bound by that law because offline and off camera, on blocks and in real hoods, Black girls operate differently, and so do these niggas.

My body has put me on the receiving end of violently hurtful fat phobia and sexism, but it has simultaneously created an opportunity for me to reconsider my gender identity, sexuality, and feminism outside the rules that had already been written for me in trap and elsewhere. When I first started to vocalize that I, too, identified as a bad bitch, many of my peers treated it as if it was satirical. They thought it was one big joke because I didn't look like the women who had been placed at the top of the fine-ass hierarchy. But my rationale was: If I was already written out of the narrative based on how I looked, then where else could I fit in, based on what I thought and what I did? What was the source of my value if it didn't come from my hip-to-waist ratio? When Rae Sremmurd said, "I don't got no type. Bad Bitches is the only thing that I like," in "No Type,"[7] I ran with it. There's room for all of us. I'm not beholden to the meanings that other people have made about my body. I'm not a trap feminist in spite of my body. I'm a trap feminist because of it.

As is the case for everyone, my body presentation dictates every part of my life. My hope is that by the end of all this you'll reconsider your own preconceived notions about what fat women can and can't do, and let it be known that bad bitches come in many different forms. As you read this book, it's important to remember that I'm not just a homegirl. I'm a fat homegirl. I wasn't just a sex worker. I was a fat sex worker. I'm not just a hood bitch. I'm a big hood bitch. And I'm not just a bad bitch. I'm a fat bad bitch.

Chapter 2

KNUCKIN', BUCKIN', READY TO FIGHT

Yeah, we knuckin' and buckin' and ready to fight!

—Crime Mob, "Knuck If You Buck"[1]

My mouth was dry as fuck. That's what I always remember about my first real fistfight. I'd scuffled with a neighborhood frenemy in second grade, but I was twelve years old now and living in the projects for the first time. I'd been in Parkway Gardens for less than a month. It was a sprawling apartment complex with a mix of buildings that were either three or eight stories tall. The entire community was gated, and there was only one way in or out. In those days, it was flanked by a Walgreens on the north, a rail yard to the west, and a skating rink called The Route on the south. Across Dr. Martin Luther King Jr. Drive to the east was an assortment of Black-neighborhood staples: corner stores, a laundromat, a motel, a church, and a restaurant with no seating and bulletproof glass separating the workers from their customers. I'd already clocked that LiLi was the HBIC of my peer group. She had a slick mouth and a slick ponytail, thin edges and all. She wasn't the prettiest girl in Parkway, but she walked around with a sense of self-assurance that I had yet to experience. She was rough around the edges. But that's what you had to be in Parkway. I'd made it a point to talk to her whenever I was outside; I wasn't exempt from her smart mouth, and I didn't back down from it either. I'd inherited my own smart-ass mouth from a mother who has her own gift of gab. It was a recipe for tension between us, and soon LiLi decided to issue a formal challenge.

We were on the side of one of the development's thirty-five buildings with a few other neighborhood kids, away from the prying eyes of grown folks and the police. LiLi stood in front of me, staring me down straight-faced before she posed the question: "You wanna fight me?" This was an ultimatum. If I said no, I'd be known as "scary," which in our language means scared of confrontation. It was bad enough I was the new bitch in the neighborhood; I couldn't be a coward too. Unfortunately, being afraid doesn't mean people leave you alone in the hood. If anything, it makes you an easier target. Had I not accepted this challenge, the dynamic between us would have always been that she pulled up on me and I didn't want the smoke. The only option was for me to stand my ground. I don't remember what I said, but I know that was the moment my mouth dried up like I'd just faced a whole blunt and had the worst cottonmouth. What was about to happen was inevitable. I didn't have time to be afraid, and even if I felt it, I couldn't dare show it.

HBIC:

Head bitch in charge. We should
all thank Tiffany "New York"
Pollard for popularizing that.

I was suddenly in motion, being pulled by my hair with one of LiLi's fists and hit in the head and face with the other. I grabbed her shirt and returned the favor. Back in the day, that was the default strategy in a girl fight: grab your opp with one hand (ideally by the hair so you also limit their eyesight and range of motion) to bring them within striking range, and hit them as hard as you can with the other. But I didn't know that at the time. I was just following her lead on how the fight was supposed to go, which, in hindsight, was my biggest mistake. I let her dictate the terms, the tone, and even the technique of the fight. She'd caught me off guard when she lashed out first, and I was continuously surprised by how tight her grip was on my hair and how forceful her punches were. I was disoriented and still trying to get my bearings. It took a few moments, but I eventually thought, *Damn, this girl is really trying to beat my ass.* This was not a game, and I realized that I needed to tip the scales in my favor. I couldn't wait for permission or some "right moment" to go hard or I was going to get my ass beat. Period. I had to "give her some go" (Chicago slang for giving someone a run for their money in a fight).

I decided to use my strength to my advantage and began yanking her toward me as hard as I could. She couldn't throw as many jabs while she struggled to stay on her feet, and that allowed me to gain some control. What had started as a small crowd had grown in the midst of all the commotion, and most of them were rooting for LiLi. I could hear their shocked reaction when I took the offensive. My strategy was working, and I had a chance to save face. Now emboldened, I began rhythmically chanting *"Bitch!"* with every blow I landed, giving the B the same energy I was putting into my wallops. That's another signature of Black girl fights that apparently comes naturally. I was confident I was gaining the upper hand until our flurry of four hands unexpectedly turned into six.

Pug was LiLi's cousin (which could have meant they were just really close friends, but I never found out), and she had jumped in to defend her. I hadn't planned on being attacked from multiple directions and had no clue what to do next. I was bigger than both of them and doing my best to keep up with their pace, but they were on a joint mission to beat me now. I could hardly see or catch my breath in the nonstop action. I started to stumble, and I knew at that moment I was losing. But I couldn't run, and I wouldn't fold, that much was clear. I eventually fell to the ground, still kicking and swinging the whole time. This was the moment I had been dreading. Here's why: There are several ways to determine who won or lost a fight. Getting stomped out on the ground, though, is the equivalent of whatever move comes after "Finish Him" on Mortal Kombat. It makes the defeat final, like Chris Tucker hovering over you as Smokey from *Friday* and announcing that "you got knocked *the fuck* out!" I fought and scrambled to get up, trying to avoid their feet at all costs. Thankfully, that moment never came because someone finally came along and broke the fight up as I frantically tried to defend myself from the ground. I'd been spared the ultimate humiliation. I certainly hadn't won, but I hadn't taken a complete L either. I'd proved to them that I was, at the very least, with the shits. I'm still proud of that to this day.

When I got up I was shaking, mouth still dry. I sauntered back to my apartment building pretending like my knees weren't trying to buckle with every step. With the adrenaline leaving my body, I physically felt the fear my brain hadn't let me acknowledge minutes ago, even though the danger was gone. In the safe solitude of the crib, where my mama and aunt had yet to hear about the altercation, I stewed in embarrassment and wondered how long I'd have to look over my shoulder walking around the complex. LiLi had been living there for years by the time I moved in, and I had way more to prove.

I was raised to be better than girls like LiLi, or to at least think I was. While LiLi and I eventually became friendly with each other, my mama often reminded me that I wasn't from the same stock as her, or some of the other girls in the complex. I was somehow being raised in the "right" way because of our family's values and care. I was meant to interpret our friendships as a matter of circumstance, not shared backgrounds and damn sure not shared futures. In many ways this was true. LiLi was always on her own or with friends, and I never met one of her parents. Meanwhile, I couldn't escape being associated with my motorcycle-riding mother. If I wasn't on the back of my mama's bike, I was piling into her blue Ford Taurus with my aunt and her two kids. LiLi cycled through the same few outfits, and they weren't always clean. My aunt went to the laundromat like clockwork, and my mama made sure our clothes were included. Plus, thanks to my solidly middle-class family members in the suburbs, I was more likely to pop up with a new pair of shoes or piece of jewelry. I was vigilant about doing my hair every day, but the gel LiLi used to slick her ponytails up into little fans was sometimes dry and flaky. One time she got cornrows and wore them until they were covered in fuzzy new growth. To pay the seven-dollar admission into juke parties at The Route, LiLi would steal disposable cameras from Walgreens and go door-to-door, selling them for five dollars a pop. I just had to beg long enough for permission to go and my mama would give me the money, plus a little extra for snacks. We were different kinds of hoodrats for sure.

The last time I saw LiLi was in 2006 during the summer before I headed off to college. My mama and I had long since left Parkway and were living in a completely different neighborhood, albeit still accessible via the 63rd Street bus. Throughout high school I'd heard stories about LiLi popping pills and selling pussy in the motel across the street from Parkway. When I saw her in my new neighborhood, she was shuffling along in my direction. After I was sure it was her, I said hello and noticed as she smiled back at me that she was missing a tooth. Growing up in intimately close proximity to addicted women, I immediately recognized the signs of her drug use. She fidgeted a little as we small-talked and reminisced about our time together as preteens. When you're eighteen, middle school feels like a lifetime ago. This was even more true for us, two young women who had clearly seen different sides of what life had to offer. Our reunion was short-lived, and before I continued on, LiLi asked the question that I could tell she'd been warming up to ask as soon as she saw me: "You got some spare change?"

Had my mama witnessed this exchange she would have used it as proof that she had been right about girls like LiLi all along. I ended up college bound and LiLi ended up strung out. But it's just not that simple. Too often we use morality, respectability, and legality to justify writing off girls like that. I know better than that now. LiLi and Pug weren't being cruel when they ran up on me, and I wasn't being bullied. I was being vetted. They needed to know I was solid and that I could and would hold my own. That's why we ended up being friendly with one another less than a month after we'd duked it out. Thanks to them, I knew what to do the next six or seven times I had to activate these hands. I'd lost the battle with LiLi and Pug, but I'd won their respect and earned the first of several stripes as the new girl on the block. Perhaps most important, I walked away from my altercation understanding the necessity of respect, self-defense, dignity, courage, and survival. The truth is that those things are worth breaking the law for, or sometimes a jaw.

*   *   *

The year of the hot girl was undeniably 2019, thanks to our good-kneed sis Megan Thee Stallion. Her catchphrase "Hot Girl Summer" caught on like wildfire. It was a seasonally specific reference to her moniker Hot Girl Meg and frequently used ad-lib: "real hot girl shit." Hot Girl Summer became such a staple that corporations and publications wasted absolutely zero time integrating it into their social media strategies. Cosmetics company Maybelline was rightfully dragged on Twitter for using the phrase in a failed attempt at Black slang. The backlash they received was a necessary moment of accountability for a big business so eager to mine Black culture for new ways to promote drugstore mascara and eyeliner. But they weren't the only ones misusing the term and watering it down to suit their tastes. Hot Girl Summer became such a huge part of the pop culture lexicon that even Megan began to offer up generalized definitions of it—like being "the life of the party" and "confident"—to keep it palatable. People were using #HotGirlSummer to describe their rosé brunches and finishing their hiking trails. Being a hot girl is about self-determination; and yes, it's great for Thee Stallion's brand that her phrases make it all the way to *The Tonight Show Starring Jimmy Fallon*. But the widespread use of Hot Girl Summer got real weird real quick.

Listeners of Thee Stallion's music know that *real* hot girl shit involves some savagery and debauchery, the things we try to shame away from Black girls for the sake of decorum. Meg's lyrical content is a cornucopia of references to female domination, rowdy confrontations, and an outright refusal to conform to other people's standards. She's not shy about what she can do with her knees, her backside, or her "thundercat." She

thot:

An invented slang word from the acronym for "that hoe over there." The term originated in Chicago and quickly spread throughout the hip-hop lexicon. Yes, it is used as a noun even though the grammar has never added up.

makes unrelenting demands for cunnilingus and coin. Based on the criteria set forth in her music, you need to be ready to throw some ass, check a bitch, and demand a check from a dude, at the very least, in order to claim hot girl status. There are plenty of women in alignment with this. Femmes flocked to social media in 2019 to share their tales of juggling multiple lovers to their benefit, videos of themselves driving the boat (drinking liquor straight from the bottle) and twerking to the beats of their own drums. "Rob him, sis," was the punch line of memes, and the idea of "CashAppiana" flourished right alongside Blueface's viral hit "Thotiana," which played on the term "thot."

During this same season, "Fuckin' on a scammin' ass, rich ass nigga"[2] could be heard from blocks away whenever groups of Black girls were congregating together. This is the line that Miami native JT delivers right before the beat drops in City Girls' single "Act Up." The single continues to enjoy mainstream success, but at its core, it's a Black girl anthem built on hood principles. For example, "I keep a baby Glock. I ain't fightin' with no random" emphasized self-defense and discernment, while "Same group of bitches. Ain't no addin' to the picture" underscored the importance of loyalty and respect. These qualities, and a little bit of finesse, are what separate real bitches from the rest. The City Girls/Hot Girl Summer of 2019 brought these girls to the front in a fresh wave of celebratory independence and joy. It was to trap bitches what the Summer of Love was to boomers. Whereas female rappers had been previously positioned as exceptions to the rule, thanks to a music industry that only invested in the success of one or two of them at a time, women abruptly took up space in the public imagination as purveyors of an indulgently renegade trap culture.

When it comes to Black girls doing their own thing for the sake of no one but themselves, though, people are definitely going to have a problem with it. Like clockwork, disapproval of the hot girl movement made itself known. The played-out argument that Black women should be aspiring to be virtuous and successful instead of fun and freaky (as if we can't be all of the above) made a home for itself in the comment sections of IG posts and nestled right into Twitter threads. As "hot girl" transformed into a phenom of uninhibited Black girl joy, one not engaged with a male gaze, I saw more people questioning if a jiggly booty was the only ingredient in Megan Thee Stallion's recipe for success—a woman who came out of the gate with harder bars than most of her male peers. JT's prison stint for fraudulent credit card charges was suddenly being used as evidence of her weak moral character and therefore undeserving of our respect or ears. The pushback was condescending but, as I mentioned, not unexpected. It was actually just another example of how misogynoir sets a different standard for us.

Trap music captures the emotional experiences and cultural nuances of trap America and honestly communicates complexities of a lifestyle that wouldn't normally be accepted

misogynoir:

A term coined by Black queer feminist Moya
Bailey in 2008 to describe the specific
form of discrimination experienced by
Black women. It combines "misogyny" and
"noir,"¹ the French word for "black."

outside the trap itself. This means that the shit just hits differently when you've lived it; and let the men tell it, lawlessness is a necessary tenet of trap music and culture. Male rappers are given the space to recount their experiences with murder, robbery, human trafficking, drug sales, drug use, obstruction of justice, and racketeering (sometimes all in the same song) and maintain all of their humanity. Every pioneering male trap artist has a story about his humble beginnings as a criminal. Somehow it has served to make them well-rounded and down-to-earth, as opposed to threatening, untrustworthy, or uncivilized. It hasn't stopped any of them from achieving mainstream success or accolades.

For example, T.I. has been arrested about ten times on a variation of drugs and weapons charges, probation violations, and, in 2018, disorderly conduct. He rebranded himself as a family-focused businessman via several reality series on BET. Another of his television endeavors includes Netflix's *Hustle & Flow*, which sees him playing a mentor role, finding up-and-coming rap talent. Gucci Mane was the dashing groom in a BET wedding special just a year after he was released from serving a two-year sentence in a federal prison for carrying a firearm as a felon. This is the same man who *still* raps about the role he played in the 2005 death of one of Jeezy's associates and selling dope well into adulthood. In 2021 he modeled in one of Beyoncé's Ivy Park campaigns. Black men have been respected and praised while they glorify their own deviance because we understand that they were surviving the hood, earning their stripes, and making a way for others. The stories of crime, not to mention the sordid details of their casual and sometimes manipulative sexcapades, are standard fare for trap niggas because they reflect the realities of many Black folks from marginalized communities.

Trap girls, on the other hand, are erased from and rewritten in those trap narratives, in ways that satisfy the egos of those men. On any given day rappers can't figure out if they prefer us over unattainable, wealthy Hilary Banks types, or "foreign" women who dote on them despite the language barriers. There are a few tributes to ghetto girls, but there are countless more references to bougie baddies who come from legitimate money. In other words, male rappers can't decide if they love the women who represent the exact opposite of who they are or those who live by the same codes as them.

To be clear, I love that entertainment is one of the few industries that allow Black folks opportunities for second (and sometimes third, fourth, and fifth) chances after being placed in the criminal justice system. You won't ever catch me questioning the success of someone because they've been incarcerated or broken some laws, especially if they were defending themselves or trying to provide for themselves and their families. Only recently in US history has the legal system been proactive about serving or protecting its most marginalized groups. And even now, people of color are disproportionately disadvantaged in the criminal justice system. To put it simply, the law has a nasty habit of fucking Black people over, so fuck the law.

I, too, tend to reject the strict codes of respectability that have been used to further police and villainize Black bodies. Chastising Black men for sagging or Black women for wearing bonnets in public or any of us for using slang isn't pushing us to Black excellence; it's internalized anti-Blackness. Ignoring the demands of the white gaze, the justice system, and cultural codes of the elite are foundations of trap culture because people from the ghetto are most affected by them; and the Black women in the trap aren't the exception. However, we're treated as such when we come up against the rules. We are expected to remain within the confines of the law, respectability, and decorum while men get to run buck fucking wild. But despite what believers in a sexist, Black utopia would like us to think, Black women aren't the gatekeepers of morality.

We haven't stayed home wringing our hands while men took to the streets to raise hell and get shit done. News of Lisa "Left Eye" Lopes burning her man's shoes, and subsequently his mansion, down; KeKe Wyatt stabbing her ex-husband; Remy Ma shooting a woman she suspected of stealing from her; Cardi B throwing a shoe at Nicki Minaj's camp during a brawl at a New York Fashion Week party; and yes, JT turning herself in to federal prison are also part of hip-hop history. Even Megan Thee Stallion has a mug shot, recently unearthed, that was the result of an altercation with her ex-boyfriend. And in our communities, where we are just as targeted for anti-Black violence and discrimination, in addition to gender-based violence, we've gotten our hands just as dirty.

I wouldn't have been able to walk to and from my own apartment building if I wouldn't have been willing to scrap with LiLi and Pug that day in Parkway, even if I was committing battery and engaged in disorderly conduct. A woman who sells her food stamps to make sure her child has school supplies or to get her hair done for a job interview is technically committing fraud. So is the woman, like my aunt when she let my mom and I live with her in Parkway, who doesn't disclose all the persons living in her apartment. Doing hair in your kitchen without a cosmetology license instead of in a salon or operating a candy store from your kitchen counter is against federal regulations. Card crackers, sex workers, and the women who beat the shit out of people who disrespect them are all breaking the law. We refuse to give up our seats on buses, we deface public property, and we flee to Cuba or just to our cousin's house two states over when the block gets too hot. Sometimes crime is the answer for us too, despite anyone's disapproval.

Let's take the infamous aforementioned feud between Cardi B and Nicki Minaj. We may never know the exact source of their beef, since interpersonal tension is often just that, personal. But while some fans chose sides based on who they thought the better MC was, and others reignited a thoughtful conversation about the fraught state of women in hip-hop, there was a vocal majority who interpreted the two women's squabbling as a failure in itself. Falling back on respectability and civility, two Black women airing out their grievances with each other represented poor taste. When the altercation spilled over from song lyrics and jabs on the internet into the elite world of high fashion, the ordeal was considered inappropriate and unacceptable. Even Nicki recounted the experience as "something so mortifying and so humiliating to go through in front of a bunch [of] upper-echelon people who have their life together. The way they passed by, looking at this disgusting commotion—I was mortified."[3]

Nicki, as did many onlookers, basically thought the whole thing was ghetto. She was embarrassed in front of the rich white folks who were nice enough to invite them both to their party. While I don't doubt that Nicki genuinely felt this way, it was interesting to witness the difference between this response and Cardi's. Both artists freely play with themes of violence—from fist-fighting to gunplay—in their music. However, Nicki has enjoyed the perks of mainstream success for about a decade longer than Cardi has. It's a position of privilege that she's had to work for and acclimate to. These two worlds—the one she made money rapping about and the one she got to access with her riches— collided at that party, and the gaze of the privileged took precedence.

Cardi, who was reported to be the aggressor in the altercation, hopped on Instagram to explain why she pulled up. (Apparently, she was under the impression that Nicki was sneak dissing her and her daughter.) It's easy to be condescending about their clash when you've never believed in a code of ethics that includes fighting in the first place, or when you've adopted the codes of a privileged majority. But Cardi was abiding by a code that demands direct confrontation over passive-aggressive politeness and cordiality. The code states that your opps can get it "on sight" and does not stipulate an appropriate time, place, or circumstance. Through this lens, their fight was unfortunate but appropriate, given their history.

I'm not writing this chapter as a trivial celebration of crime, immorality, or violence. However, the lawlessness of the trap deserves a closer look so that we can recognize the common thread running through all of the circumstances I just mentioned: hood anarchy is often a response to poverty, danger, an unreliable justice system, and a lack of resources. We fight because we can't trust the law to settle disputes for us. We sell shit under the table to make ends meet when we're not paid enough. We redistribute what we have to the family members and friends the government has deemed "unqualified" for the same benefits.

When I think about my family's adamancy that I don't end up like LiLi—or some of my other homegirls who've spent their lives trying to raise kids without so much as a GED, let alone a college education; those who've never had their mental health issues taken seriously or diagnosed; those experiencing intimate partner violence; or even those who never met a college graduate until I got my bachelor's—I know what makes us different. Nothing else separates me from LiLi, or Cardi from Nicki, except opportunity and resources.

* * *

I was nineteen years old the first time I was arrested. It was a year after that last time I'd run into LiLi, and I was back in the city after my first dismal year of college. I'd brought all my clothes, vibrators, and a heavy Dell laptop back in big plastic storage bins and quickly found a job working at Borders bookstore. In addition to my barely passing GPA, I'd also returned home with a newfound skill: shoplifting. I'd started stealing from stores because I was broke and didn't know how to budget the little bit of money I was making from my work-study program. If I needed a new pair of jeans or shoes and didn't have an extra twenty to fifty dollars lying around, I'd just take it. The same was true for food and other household needs, like body wash. When I realized that I was actually good at stealing, shit changed.

In hindsight (it's been over a decade since I've stolen anything), I know now that I was getting off on the power of it all. I liked having access to things I couldn't afford, finessing people around me to see what I wanted them to see, and being successful at *something*. I was at the very beginning of adulthood, and none of that shit was going how I thought it would. I wasn't nearly as grown as I thought I was. I'd damn near failed out of school in the first year but was still too proud to consider changing my major from biology to something that suited my skills as a communicator and critical thinker. I was overdrawing my checking account every time I got paid and had no idea where my life was headed. Every time I made it out of a store with something I hadn't paid for felt like a win. *Something* was going right for me.

I could go into a store with friends who were actually spending money, walk out with a ton of shit I'd stolen, and they wouldn't have a clue until we were in the car headed home. Sometimes I'd buy a couple of items and triple the amount of stuff in my bag. I made sure that I interacted with the staff. In department stores, I would chat up sales associates, sometimes with merchandise in my hand where they could see it. Even if the loss-prevention folks had pinged me as suspicious when I walked in, I imagined them relaxing and moving on to someone else after seeing me cozied up with their sales associate Barb in the plus-size section. Most important, I followed my instincts. If I ever had an inkling that someone was onto me, I was comfortable putting every item back on the shelf and abandoning the mission. But my biggest advantage was that I knew how to look "like a shopper." This is partly because I'd worked in retail since I was a teenager. But it's also because I had certain advantages that other Black girls did not.

Even if my grades sucked and I was only a year removed from living in the middle of active gang territory, I was now a student at one of the best public-research institutions in the country. I was better at code switching in a way that could both impress and disarm white folks. My clothes didn't always work for my shape or my comfort, but I only occasionally dressed in anything that was immediately off-putting or screamed hoodrat. As much as I could as a fat Black girl, I fit in, which is a privilege in itself.

When I was arrested in 2007, which was the first and only time I ever got caught stealing, it wasn't because I got lazy or fell off my game. I was committed to my normal routine, but I carelessly introduced an unpredictable element into the formula: a friend. As more of my squad realized how successful I'd become at boosting, they wanted to take advantage. They'd make requests for themselves or their loved ones, and suddenly I had an opportunity to make a few bucks on the side. I was no longer shopping for myself when I went on these trips, but I *was* usually shopping for women, which is probably why when one of my male friends wanted some clothes from Nordstrom on Michigan Avenue for free ninety-nine, we decided we'd go in together.

Now seems like a good time to make a point of clarification. It really is a coincidence that my first legitimate job in high school a few years earlier was at the same Nordstrom. I'd shopped there in the years since, and yes, I'd stolen from them just a few weeks before this fateful day. But I hadn't cased them out in advance to make this a more sophisticated hit. They were just as fair game as the Neiman Marcus down the street. Just in case some of my old Nordstrom coworkers are reading this, it's important that I set the record straight.

Anyway, my friend Mark was excited about our little adventure on my off day, but he was not a booster or any other kind of criminal. He went to high school in the suburbs and came from a good, two-parent home. He was skinny, attractive, super into fashion, but always single. Most of our mutual friends, and I, were just waiting for the day when he'd feel comfortable enough to come out as queer. My family loved him because he was mannerable and they knew he'd never get me pregnant. He really was a "good" boy. Here's the thing about good boys, though. They're usually bitch niggas. As harsh as it sounds, I mean it in the most respectful way. They're not cut out for criminal activity beyond underage drinking or buying a quarter ounce from the local weed man, and this works for them because they usually stay in their lane. They go to college, finally have sex, drink some more, graduate, get a good job, travel with their friends or girlfriends, never improve at sex, get married, get promoted, make a decent living for themselves, have some kids, and get old content that they did life the right way. If they're queer, things might get a little spicy, but the general trajectory is still the same. They work best aboveboard, aren't great under pressure, and can't really finesse because they don't have to. They're not city boys or hot boys, and they're definitely not scammin' ass, rich ass niggas. Mark was not an exception.

Once we were inside the store, I was committed to my normal routine of looking like a regular young woman trying to figure out how to spend the money she earned at her retail job on unnecessary clothing. Mark and I talked and joked as if nothing were going on. I held up items that I thought he might like and even bagged a couple of things for one of my homegirls. I only had to tell him to relax, or tell him when to sneak something into my bag, a couple of times. But he was nervous, and I was arrogant about our ability to blend in. I assumed that Mark, my scrawny, clean-cut, square friend, made us look more inconspicuous. And while I wasn't watching the monitors to know what tipped security off to our malfeasance, I imagine it was his shiftiness, or perhaps our playful energy in an otherwise stuffy retailer. Our individual privileges aside, two young Black people who obviously weren't a couple weren't necessarily low-key. Either way, I should have left his frail ass at home. In the seventy-two hours after the loss-prevention team asked us to accompany them to their office, and held us there until the police arrived, I regretted that more and more.

Nothing makes the disparities of class, race, and gender more explicit than navigating law enforcement and the criminal justice system. It was clear very early on that Mark's and my university IDs weren't going to get the Nordstrom security to let us go in an act of kindness. In addition to around seven hundred dollars' worth of merchandise, they'd also found in my bag a special screwdriver used to pop security tags, and one of the male guards remembered me from my time as an employee. They'd watched us for a while and waited until we were about to leave the store just to confirm what we were up to. They'd marked me as a professional and weren't even swayed by

Mark's fearful, cracking voice when he insisted we weren't *that* kind of people. To them, we were exactly that kind of people, both of us. I actually respect the employees for that, for treating Mark and me as equals, because the annoyed officer who arrived to take us to jail only wanted to arrest me. Mark had pocketed a fake gold necklace worth about forty dollars, but the bag with most of the stolen merchandise in it was mine. Even though most of the clothes were men's and in Mark's size, the officer was only concerned with which charges were most likely to stick. Plus, he would have to call backup since Mark would need to be transported to a men's holding facility and I to a women's. The white woman working for Nordstrom grew flustered as she explained that her team saw Mark put items into my bag, and insisted on the officer doing his job. She knew that I was stealing for my friend, and even though she wouldn't spare me, she damn sure wouldn't let me go down for it alone. God bless her for that, I guess.

But after we were escorted out in cuffs, Mark and I had completely different experiences in the fallout of our stealing spree. Here's how the law works regarding shoplifting in Illinois: It's a misdemeanor crime if the merchandise or property amounts to less than three hundred dollars. Anything more than that is considered a felony. Mark was only charged with taking the forty-dollar chain, booked, and released a few hours after the whole ordeal started. Because I was the one in possession of the bag with everything else, I was being held accountable for everything else. Charged with a felony, I had to go before a judge to have a bond hearing the next day. I called a friend to let them know what was going on (which is how I found out Mark was already out) and spent the night alone in a holding cell.

The following morning, I was aggressively catcalled through glass in the paddy wagon where I and a couple of other female detainees were separated from the men. The same thing happened as we were escorted through the bowels of the infamous Cook County Jail, past bullpens of male detainees waiting for judges to determine (via video chat) where they'd be spending the foreseeable future. This was a spectacular display of inappropriate male bravado, considering I hadn't showered, brushed my teeth, washed my face, done my hair, or slept in over twenty-four hours. At least the other women in our bullpen were more helpful. They insisted I'd be let out on a personal recognizance bond and wouldn't have to pay a thing. This was music to my ears, as my primary concern during that time was making sure my mama didn't find out my ass was in jail. She thought I'd just spent the night with a friend. When the judge surprised everyone and set my bail at $20,000 (which meant I had to come up with $2,000), I had to spend another night in jail, this time in Cook County Jail.

I thought the first night after I was arrested was shitty, but being processed into jail after my bond hearing is one of the life experiences I've tried my damnedest to forget. The processing center was a huge room filled with mostly people of color, fluorescent lighting, body odor, and lots of noise. I was shuffled to one station to have a "mental health evaluation," then off to another part of the room to be fingerprinted. I signed a few papers along the way, overwhelmed with how little control I had over my life at that point. There would be no finessing or code-switching here because it was no one's job in this room to give a damn about who I was or why I was there. The general vibe was that most of the women there, an overwhelming number of whom were Black, had done this before and knew what to expect. I did not.

When I got to the picture station, I lost my balance as I tried to stand where the white male officer needed me to be. I didn't fall, but I reflexively looked down at my feet to make sure I hadn't tripped over anything right as my picture was being taken. As a result, only half my face was visible in the already grainy photo. "Stupid bitch!" the officer spat at me as if I'd ruined *his* day. From there I was strip-searched and required to bend over, spread my ass cheeks, and cough. When I finally got a chance to shower, I did so with a group of female strangers while female officers watched. My clothes and belongings were taken and swapped for a pair of white drawers and a dull bluish-green uniform to wear that felt like paper. I was handed a bag with a blanket, a toothbrush, and some other shit I can't remember before I was rounded up into yet another big holding cell.

I made another call to my friend, who finally reached Mark via three-way, to see if they could crowdfund two grand for me. They weren't hopeful about it, but it was my last resort since I still didn't want to tell my mother—the only person who could actually help me—where I was. I would be spending another night in jail, and I was running out of steam after nearly thirty hours without sleep. I ended up falling into a nap on the dirty floor surrounded by about twenty other women. When I was finally assigned to a bed, not even the sound of mice scurrying around the walls or the itchy fabric of the blanket could keep me awake.

The next day I had a terrible excuse for breakfast and another opportunity to make a phone call. I knew it was time to finally bite the bullet and call my mama. "Why are you in jail, Sesali?!" was the first thing she said to me since an automated voice had already announced where I was calling collect from. I don't remember the details of the rest of conversation, but it ended with the reassurance that she was coming to get me. I can't say that was necessarily a relief, though. The weight of how badly I'd fucked up hit me all at once. After I hung up, I cried for the first time. Sometimes the weight of your situation doesn't hit you until you hear the hurt, disappointment, and fear in your parent's voice.

Here's something else you need to know about being thrown in jail: Once you're behind those bars, you're not a person. You're a number. Your background, identity, and privileges don't matter once you're locked up. But they definitely matter in the process of getting you out.

Bail actually wasn't the first option for my release. No one wanted to spend $2,000 if they didn't have to. Because I was a first-time, nonviolent offender, I was eligible for a furlough release. Under this provision, I would be able to wear an ankle monitor and travel for work (I'd already called out "sick" to Borders for one day) and other essential functions until my official court date. So long as there was a residence with a working phone line, I was eligible. Having a loved one who gave a damn about me not spending another night in jail—and having a place to house me—was a privilege I'd definitely taken for granted until that moment. When the furlough was approved, I was called out of the housing unit, given back my clothes, put into my electronic monitoring device, and finally driven to the apartment I shared with my mom. I couldn't wait to take a private shower and sleep comfortably. But unfortunately, the sheriff couldn't set up whatever technology they needed to keep tabs on me because of shoddy phone wiring in our apartment. Just like that, I was ineligible for the furlough and taken right back to jail. Someone was going to have to come up with that two grand. With the same reluctance I'd had when it was time for me to confess to her that I was in jail, my mama called *her* mama, my granny, and told her what was happening. Together, the women in my family gathered up the money to get me home for good.

I called Mark several times when I got home to update him on what was going on, find out how he was doing, and figure out what our next steps would be. Despite our different ordeals with the law, I still thought we were in the shit together and that he was worried about me. He didn't answer any of my calls. After three days of this, I knew he was avoiding me, which hurt me, but it pissed my mama off even more. She loved Mark, we'd gone to high school dances together, he always had been around, and she'd grown to trust him. As upset as she was with me, she couldn't just let his betrayal go. It was her idea to pull up on him at his parents' house and confront him about his disappearing act. He answered the door of their quaint single-family home in one of the affluent neighborhoods on the South Side, and looked like he was about to shit bricks at the sight of us. I immediately knew that his parents had no clue what their only son had been up to. When we told them what had happened, they were not only disappointed that he'd been stealing but also upset that he would turn his back on his homegirl after she had caught a case trying to help him be fresh. The bitch nigga really jumped out of Mark and now even his parents knew it. I don't think I have to spell it out, but shit was never the same between us.

With that out of the way, though, I was still facing a felony and didn't have the backing of a well-to-do family to help me out of it. What I did have was a mama who was a hustler and had her own network of associates who'd faced charges way more serious than mine. They referred her to a defense attorney who had a reputation in the hood for securing best-case scenarios in situations way more serious than mine. Again, she crowdfunded the money from my family, and I pitched in what I could from my part-time checks to make sure he was paid. This was another privilege of mine, a family that could figure it out. I didn't really fuck with the lawyer because he didn't bother with the details of my case or my life until the day of my actual hearing. On days when he would pull up to our apartment in his Benz to collect checks through the window, he'd repeatedly ask me if I'd had any prior arrests or convictions, because he couldn't remember the answer I'd given him the last time. He clearly had bigger fish to fry, but that didn't stop him from keeping excellent records of how much we'd paid him leading up to my court date. I finished out my summer as if nothing had happened. I kept working at Borders and was there the night hundreds of people lined up outside our store to be the first to get their hands on a copy of *Harry Potter and the Deathly Hallows*.

On the day of my hearing, my mother and I woke up early to head to the courthouse. We watched several other cases get resolved in our assigned courtroom, waiting for my out-of-touch lawyer to arrive. When he finally showed up, he asked me *again* if I'd had any other arrests and to remind him of which university I was a student at. If I wasn't so preoccupied with the fact that my future was in someone else's hands, I would have rolled my eyes at him. He told me that he knew this judge, describing him as "tough but fair." He was hoping to have me convicted of a misdemeanor retail theft and put on supervision, which would have the whole thing wiped off my record for good after a period of time. When he presented on my behalf, he made sure to name-drop my school and referred to me as a "good kid" multiple times.

Representatives from Nordstrom had shown up to the

hearing as well, and as "victims" of the crime they got to have a say-so in what happened to me. My stomach felt like it was vibrating in my body as they convened with my lawyer at the judge's bench, out of earshot from me. Watching other defendants be brought in and taken out in handcuffs had sent my mind hurtling toward a worst-case scenario that I hadn't even considered: I could be sent back to jail. Even if it was only for two more days, it would have been too much for me. My mouth was dry as the parties dispersed back to their respective places in the courtroom, which now felt to me like a big sepia tomb.

I held my breath as the judge started to speak. Nordstrom had agreed to sticking me with only a misdemeanor. I exhaled, hoping that the judge's sentencing would also bring good news. But when my lawyer said the judge was tough, he meant it. I wasn't granted supervision—I was sentenced to two years of probation and a restitution fee. Then I was given a short lecture about returning to college, the judge saying, "You've got a great opportunity in front of you. Don't ruin it with stupid stuff." I left the courtroom that day with weak knees, a criminal record, and feeling like a white man had equated the college education I was paying for with some kind of free handout.

As I fulfilled the terms of my probation, which thankfully didn't involve in-person visits or drug testing, I was grateful for how all those small privileges had added up for me. A loving, resourceful family, college enrollment, housing security, and even sound mental health all made it so I could advocate for myself at key moments. Shit could have been worse. But it also could have been better. About four years later I had an English class with a white girl from one of the north suburbs who shared her story about being arrested for shoplifting. She immediately had been placed in a diversion program where she took a few classes, never faced a conviction, and didn't have a criminal record. When I talked to her after class, she said she hadn't spent a minute in jail. They'd taken her information and sent her home, and she'd received orders to report to the program in the mail.

Do I feel bad that Walmart, Nordstrom, or Macy's may have missed out on a couple thousand bucks on my behalf? Not really. Do I think it was stupid for me to risk my freedom and future for a few hundred bucks or some new outfits? Absolutely, because I understand both my privileges *and* the ways in which I'm marginalized. Crime isn't unique to Black people or Black communities. Google "serial killers" or "white collar crime" or "Fyre Fest" or "school shooters" or "college admissions scam" to see what I mean. However, for a group that is disenfranchised under the guise of the law, crime can be a radical part of how we survive and effect change in our lives.

*   *   *

When people joke that "Knuck If You Buck" is an old Negro spiritual, they're referencing the surge of emotion and adrenaline Black folks feel when it comes on. The Crime Mob track about throwing elbows, punches, and shots (knucking) is a war cry that evokes feelings of pride, fearlessness, aggression, and defiance (in other words, the state of being buck). These are the feelings that Black people get killed for expressing elsewhere, under a sexist, white supremacist, heterosexual, imperialist regime. Now the unified meeting of fists and open hands, which has become the unofficial dance move to accompany "Knuck If You Buck," will likely become part of our ancestral muscle memory. It's an artistic expression of resistance, resilience, and authenticity, and my favorite example of what author and professor LaMonda Horton-Stallings called the "Black ratchet imagination,"[4] in which themes that are assumed irresponsible and unproductive within American culture actually reflect our creative potential. What has always made the song supremely special to me, though, is what happens to Black girls when Princess, one of the group's two female members, enters the song. "Yeah, we knuckin' and buckin' and ready to fight!" We get loud, the function gets even more hyped, and suddenly the song is ours. It's a recognition of Black femme power, Black femme aggression, Black femme fearlessness, and Black femme defiance.

Today's female rap scene is so inspiring because it's thriving off this raw realness. When Rico Nasty thanks God that she didn't have to smack a bitch today, she's creatively channeling what Audre Lorde called "uses of anger."[5] All at once it's an acknowledgment of our oppression and the control we have over our own circumstances, however limited they may be. And when Asian Doll admits the sex was so good that she came twice, but she's still not loving the dick or the trick, she's subverting the inherent power assigned to men under hetero-patriarchy. All are talking about putting their foot up bitches' asses and disrespecting these niggas. The continued success of these women is a sign that we're going to do what the fuck we want to do anyway. These are modern, creative responses that can be applied not only to racism but to misogynoir, or the particular way in which Black women experience oppression.

Trap feminism is not about setting the LiLis apart from anyone else. It's about acknowledging the power and potential they already have, just as they are. I'm different from LiLi in a lot of ways, but we're also the same type of bitch: real. We both had to throw those punches that day. When a trap feminist uses that Laurel Thatcher Ulrich quote that everyone loves, "Well-behaved women seldom make history,"[6] she's not talking about wearing pussy hats or whistle-blowing sexism at a corporation. Sometimes the misbehaved women are lying about where they live to give their child a better shot at an education, stealing clothes and selling them to their friends, or stabbing the nigga who tries to push up on them during their walk home from work. We do what we have to when we can't do what we want to.

Chapter 3

FIVE-STAR BITCH

Still that bitch . . . will forever be that bitch.

—Megan Thee Stallion, "Savage"[1]

Confidence is a touchy subject for me, and not because I lack any. I am, for the most part, very okay with who I am, what I have, and what I look like. When I'm naked in front of the mirror, I see a body, one of the billions of bodies taking up space on this Earth. There are things I don't like about my body, and my life in general, but there are a lot more things that I do. That's what confidence looks like for me these days. But when *other* people call me "confident," that's when I start feeling some type of way.

If you're reading this and you've never been fat, let me ask you a question: How often are you called confident? Perhaps during a therapy session? Maybe you overheard your mother or auntie bragging about you to someone else and they commended you for always going after the things you want and believing with all your heart that you could achieve them. If you have super-supportive homegirls, I can see it coming up during a particularly validating kiki over drinks. But have you ever been doing something completely normal, like dancing at a party, walking into a venue dolled up for an event or date, or just competently doing your job, and had a total stranger (or even a casual acquaintance) commend you for being *sooooo confident*? People may have complimented you on your beauty, your outfit, your hair, your perspective, your talent. But has anyone offered you, a person who is not fat, a read on how you must feel about *yourself* on a day-to-day basis? Probably not.

That happens to me, a fat Black girl, all the time. I'll be minding my own business and some woman will find her way over to me, from across the room, just to say, "Girl, I wish I had your confidence!" I'm rolling my eyes just thinking about it. It's annoying, presumptuous, kind of invasive, and a bit nonsensical. Let's just call a spade a spade here: calling me confident is a backhanded compliment loaded with connotations about how other people think I should be presenting myself to the world.

People call me confident when they think I look good, seem happy, or sound smart, but they've internalized those qualities as contradictions to my fatness and Blackness. What people who call me confident are trying to do is work through their own discomfort with my body and make sense of the fact that I don't appear to share in that discomfort. That I'm not visibly debilitated by the weight of my body and our culture's fat phobia is triggering for folks. They think I should be operating from a deficit of confidence, that insecurity should be oozing out of my pores, and that I shouldn't be able to impress them in any capacity. But I do. In this context, my perceived confidence feels grandiose at best, if not downright delusional. There was a memo sent out about girls like me, and I missed it. That I refuse to hide myself, and instead choose to enjoy my life, is interpreted as just as excessive as my body. Doing well, in any sense of the word, has become an open invitation for people to evaluate my self-esteem. What people who call me confident sometimes mean is that if they looked like me, or came from where I came from, they would be trying to crawl into the nearest hole and die there. The fact that I dare come outside with this body, let alone dress it up in a cute outfit, laugh, smile, dance, take a fire ass picture of it, and call myself a bad bitch is astonishing to people who have invested in the idea that my body is on the bottom of the totem pole.

Then there are the other fat women who see me writing about being fat, speaking at events and on panels about being fat, posting those fire ass pictures of my fat body for all of my followers to see, and using the word "fat" to describe my body. They've experienced the same shame, disdain, and policing that I have. They, like me, want to glow up anyway. They also think I have "larger-than-life" confidence, because they know how hard it is to simply exist. I'm not annoyed when they ask me for advice on how to be more comfortable with themselves. I'm hurt and pissed off at the world on their behalf. I have to break the news to them that my confidence is not larger-than-life. I have to tell them that the fat phobia and mistreatment persists, no matter what I say or how many crop tops I wear. Confidence is a choice, and not an easy one. It's the choice between crying about it and smiling anyway. In some ways it *is* a delusion, because there are certainly days when there's absolutely nothing to laugh about. It's also a painful process that requires honesty and work. Confidence is waiting on the other side of choosing to keep it real with yourself, choosing to heal some shit, choosing to humble yourself. It pisses me off when people call me confident for being fine, funny, smart, or joyous because the seeds of my confidence were actually planted and watered when I was unraveling, depressed, and deeply unhappy.

Throughout middle school, high school, and a big chunk of college I was in defense mode. Not only was I the fat girl; I also came from a family that was, during that time, fractured. My mom was an addict who loved me deeply and did her best to make sure I was taken care of. But she certainly had her own share of shit to deal with. My adolescence was profoundly affected by the instability of a parent who was driven by both her addiction and a sincere desire to do better. When she'd start another stint in rehab, or was experiencing housing instability, I'd be sent to live with my family in the suburbs. In the back-and-forth, I constantly transferred schools. Fun fact: I attended nine schools before college, one of which I transferred back into after leaving for a time. What I learned to do in the midst of all that constant moving around and starting over was to keep up the appearance at all costs. There was no time or space for me to feel the impact of my circumstances emotionally. No one ever asked me if I was okay, and I never talked to a therapist about any of it. My perseverance was the only measure of success. By any means necessary, I was supposed to keep going. I was expected to go to school, get good grades, and stay on track to make something of myself. I had to "fix my face" while I was at it, which in Black households means no crying or moping around. At that time, the most powerful tool at my disposal was my adaptability. It was the only thing I had control over, and I was damned good at it.

My survival rested in my ability to make friends, fit in, and navigate the social hierarchy of teenagers. I knew when to be tough and when to crack jokes. I was loud and extra, and found that I could easily disarm people with my personality (which is part of the reason I was so good at boosting later on in life). I easily made friends with everyone: the cheerleaders, the queer kids, the weed smokers, and the unfriendly hotties who were misunderstood by everyone else. I made myself emotionally impenetrable and projected an effortless air of not giving a fuck. Either you liked me or you didn't. And if you were part of the latter group, you at least knew enough about me to understand that I was with all the shits and not one to try.

I mastered the art of keeping calm and carrying on, and I knew how and who to finesse. I always knew how to react, and I had lots to say, but the truth is that I was hardly processing anything substantial about my life. I lived life day by day and moment by moment. Because all of my energy was focused outward, I wasn't tending to my spiritual, mental, or emotional state at all. I didn't feel confident. I also didn't feel insecure. I generally felt very little except a need to stay in the game.

boosting:

Another word for stealing that is
typically reserved for those who turn a profit
on their stolen merchandise. Example: For as
much as these boosters are charging, I can
just buy the shit from the store at full price!

When I got to college, though, my circumstances changed faster than I even realized it was happening. My friends, many of whom I'd known since middle school, started naturally evolving, growing into the people they were meant to be. Meanwhile, I was still hyper-focused on trying to present myself to everyone else in a way that would dictate how they reacted to me, but I wasn't being myself because I didn't really know who the fuck that was. I wanted to seem exceptional without being exceptional, and at least a few people could see right through it.

Facebook used to have this feature called an Honesty Box where people could submit anonymous comments to you, and you could choose to make them public and respond to them. It was a weird way of normalizing trolling, because the assumption was that the comments were only going to be from people you actually knew. The only clue it would give you about the person's identity was either a blue box if the commenter was male or a pink one if they were female. This is way before Facebook offered nonbinary gender options for its users. Anyway, I remember getting quite a few of them, most of them harmless jokes from friends of mine. But the only one I still remember, over a decade later, is one that said: *You use humor to hide the fact that you're uncomfortable about your weight!* Or something like that. Naturally, I was ready to clap the fuck back. I said: *No, my weight makes YOU uncomfortable, not me. I'm just funny, and a bad bitch* . . . Or something like that.

But this interaction has always stuck with me, because years later I realized that the commenter had been right. I was using a cocktail of humor, toughness, and literal volume to hide my vulnerabilities. I may have thought I had mastered it, but some people could see right through my act and thought I was just fucking obnoxious. I got over on a lot of people by selling them on how cool and interesting I was because I was scared shitless to show most people my weaknesses or inadequacies. My face always had to be "fixed," lest I feel the gravity of what I'd been through. I thought that to respond to my inner turmoil meant a certain end of the world as I knew it. I'd figured out how to get by, because I thought that if I didn't, it would mean I somehow was failing at life. But the gag is that I was failing at life anyway.

Fall 2009 should have been the first semester of my last year of college. But I had been pulling off a passable GPA for only about a year and a half at that point. I'd initially been too stubborn to change my major from a science and pre-med focus (what I thought I *should* think was important) to something more suited to my blossoming interests in writing, social justice, and Black girl culture (the shit I *actually* thought was important). For the first two years of undergrad, I was on academic probation pretty much every semester. I often had to write appeals at the end of each term with sob stories about some hardship I didn't actually face in order to keep my financial aid or remain in good standing with the university.

During the second half of my sophomore year I decided I could settle on sociology as a suitable major. A year later, I stopped resisting and changed my major again to gender and sexuality studies, which turned out to be the perfect fit. Thanks to a graduate level course with the brilliant Dr. Ruth Nicole Brown, I'd also become involved in SOLHOT (Saving Our Lives, Hear Our Truths), which is a celebration of Black girlhood that takes on many shapes and forms. I was involved as one of the adult volunteers (we're called "homegirls") who helped organize and facilitate a space for preteen Black girls (they're called "lil homies") to express themselves through art, storytelling, and community. Almost all of our lil homies were from the local working-class community surrounding our university. They were literally and figuratively from "the other side of the tracks," but unlike other advocacy-based groups that ventured into their neighborhoods in hopes of doing community service or outreach, SOLHOT wasn't interested in an interventionist or risk-aversion approach to dealing with Black girls. We weren't there because we thought Black girls were too loud, too ghetto, uncivilized, or in desperate need of someone to stop them from getting pregnant. SOLHOT reveled in the resilience, defiance, and attitudes of Black girls. We wanted them to talk back and make meaning of their own lives, not have someone else come in and do it for them. I knew how important it was for them to have space where that was possible. I didn't realize how badly I also needed that space.

By my junior year, I was finally pulling As and Bs in my courses and slowly raising my pathetic GPA. But I'd had to work at it nonstop. I'd attended summer school every year after sophomore year, and by fall 2009, I knew that graduating with my peers the following spring wasn't going to happen. Plus, I was still trying to figure out how to pay my rent, utilities, car note, car insurance, and phone bill. I couldn't easily apply for jobs because I had a fresh retail theft on my criminal record. Whatever little bit of extra money I had I was blowing on the worst weed rural America had to offer, fast food, and gas for Sandy. When it came to groceries and other necessities, I had to temporarily reactivate my skills as a thief.

My mama had gotten clean for good and had started to re-build her life by the time I went to college. Midway through the education they were so proud of me for pursuing, my family was reconnecting in ways I had never seen before, and I didn't really feel part of that closeness. I felt further and further away from them as my college years rolled on. My poor academic performance and recent arrest meant my life was moving in a direction and at a pace I knew they wouldn't approve of. I didn't know how to bridge that gap between us because I had never learned how to open up channels of communication for hard conversations, and perhaps they didn't either. They found out about my life on a material, tragedy-by-tragedy basis: like when the car that my mama cosigned for me to get was at risk of re-possession, or when I was behind on rent, or when I was leaving the university they'd dropped me off at three years earlier and returning home with no degree in hand.

I could open up to my friends, but we were also headed in different directions. My peers were traveling, having meaningful relationships, and actively trying to become fully formed adults. They were graduating and entering the workforce. I wasn't even bothering to submit applications for part-time jobs if I knew they would do a background check. They were having new experiences, while I was procrastinating and depressed. A serious breaking point came when my best friend decided that she needed space from me because my immaturity and lack of accountability were becoming too much for her. She was, and still is, the person I've counted on for unwavering acceptance and understanding. Even if it did last for only a week, it broke my heart that she'd decided she was over me. With even my closest friendships at risk, I felt alone for the first time ever.

I'd been to therapy a few times during my first couple of years in college. When I completed a transfer to another university after blowing it at the first one, and no longer had health insurance, I started a meditation practice that seriously shifted something in me. I was pushed toward honesty and authenticity. I started being intentional about how I spent time with people. I learned how to shut the fuck up and listen to other people, and to myself. I was peeling back layers, and I realized that I was carrying a lot of trauma and resentment from my childhood. I was finally willing to do more than brag about my war wounds; I was remembering how much they hurt and how scared and sometimes angry I was when I got them. I wasn't damaged, but I was damn sure wounded. Apologies were owed to me, and I owed some of my own.

The person in my Honesty Box had been right about the fact

that so much of my life was a facade, but it wasn't because of my weight. It was from years of repression, a lack of stability, surviving abuse, and my own sense of failure. When I started to acknowledge those underlying issues, I actually felt *more* comfortable in my own skin. I'd learned from SOLHOT that I could be any version of Black girl I wanted to be, so long as I kept it a buck. All the talk about being a bad bitch was starting to materialize in a deeper way.

The six years I spent as an undergraduate student were simultaneously the best and the worst years of my life. But as with everything, there are levels to this shit, and those were just the first steps to building the confidence I have now. My journey with confidence has been like a swinging pendulum. It started at one extreme end in my childhood and early teen years, where I hated what I saw in the mirror, tried to avoid the topic of my own fatness like the plague, and ignored the darker realities of my home life. In college, it swung to the other extreme end, where I bragged about being a hood bitch and offered my body up to the world without discernment just to convince people I was impenetrable. The latter was a move that sometimes set me up for mistreatment, and in some cases violence, because I still wasn't really in touch with my own humanity. It wasn't until I really committed to healing, and not just getting by, that I started to strike the necessary balance.

It's not exceptional that I think I'm beautiful, or that I'm self-assured enough to walk into a room with my head held high. Setting boundaries and demanding the respect I'm owed by virtue of being a grown ass woman are just part of what it means to be a fully formed human. There's nothing larger than life about that. It's a human right, a state of being that everyone is entitled to. When people call me confident, they say it as if I've somehow cheated the system, like it's a steal. I'm not "lucky" for not hating myself. Suffering is not and should not be the punishment for not being perfect. You deserve help if you need it, whether it's in the form of therapy, a more supportive community, self-affirmations, journaling, bodywork, makeup tutorials, self-care, or whatever. Too many people are made to feel like they somehow haven't earned the right to be okay with themselves. If you're one of those people, I'm here to tell you that you have. You have permission to be satisfied with who you are, what you look like, and what you have. You also have permission to take your time, and as many times as it takes, to figure it out according to the changing circumstances in your life.

* * *

Now . . . if you're only interested in figuring out how to feel better about yourself, we're done here. You have my advice on how to be more confident and you can go ahead and skip to the next chapter. But that's not the real tea. The real tea is that confidence doesn't make me a bad bitch. When you're big, built bad, queer, and a little hood like me, confidence alone isn't going to get you the things you want or take you to the places you want to go. Standards and morals will. Confidence can keep you afloat and keep you away from self-loathing, self-harm, and other kinds of despair. But in my experience, having strong personal standards is the only way to level up. "Strong" is a vital part of that sentence because standards are almost useless if you're not willing to enforce and hold them.

I had all of these ideas about the type of person I was: I was a real bitch. I was sexually liberated. I was a feminist. I was a good friend. I was cute. I was ambitious and on my way to certain success. I was all about my money. As I struggled to find confidence in these years, I doubled down on these traits and made sure that I was always loud about them. I talked a good talk, and in some ways, walked the walk. For example, I almost immediately figured out ways to make feminism a foundational principle in my life, dictating the kinds of jobs and volunteer work I did. But on other fronts, all I had were strong opinions and nothing to show for them.

I've already told you what was happening with my grades and how my money management was going. So all that stuff about success and money was bullshit. I was also fucking people I wasn't necessarily attracted to, or, at the very least, people who didn't deserve a single piece of pussy from me. (And faking orgasms with them! Ew.) I also wasn't showing up for my friends in the ways they needed me to. I had a decent sense of style, but I wasn't investing in my appearance at all. I'd reached a place where I felt like I could claim the things I thought I deserved. But I wasn't doing any of the work to attain them. I thought I was channeling the energy I've always loved in female rappers. That *I'm a bad bitch and I run this shit* energy. But all I had done was set the standards. I wasn't actually respecting them, and it showed.

The message to Black girls, and especially to fat Black girls, or Black girls from the hood, is that we're supposed to take what we can get. It's a message that not only devalues us but also keeps us conveniently in the service of people who would seek to have power over us. For example, if Black girls are supposed to take what they can get in their relationships, why should they hold their partners accountable when they're toxic? If Black girls are supposed to take what they get in the job market, why would they question making only 62 cents to a white man's dollar? Thanks to my feminism, and years of being confident, I'd started to reject these ideas . . . in theory. But I hadn't interrogated how I'd also internalized those messages and was holding myself back. As a result, I would spend many more years with *just* confidence. But I wanted alignment in my life and wanted to make sure that I was walking the walk. I knew I valued myself, and I couldn't figure out why other people didn't seem to value me too. It turns out it's because I was making too many concessions. I thought that as long as I was loud about how confident I was, people would hear me and fall in line. It doesn't work like that. I had to show them how I wanted to be treated.

bougie:

Derived from the French word "bourgeois,"
it is reserved for Black people with refined
tastes and mannerisms (or those who think
they have them). The implication is often
that these tastes are above the station
or birth of the person who holds them.

Maintaining your standards means saying no to people, places, and things that don't serve you. Here's a petty ass example: at this age I don't go to clubs unless I'm invited, I have somewhere to sit down, and I don't have to wait in line for entry or drinks. I can count the number of times that I've made exceptions to this rule on one hand. (One of them was Frank Ocean's first PrEP+ party in 2019, and it was worth it.) This usually means paying extra for bottle service, and I've declined invites when no one else was willing to pay the extra money. Similarly, I don't like traveling on a tight budget. I want to be able to buy some art, get a massage, eat wherever I want, and do whatever I want when experiencing a new place. I also need a comfortable place to sleep at the end of the night. Does this make me bougie? No. I've just learned to prioritize my own comfort.

Holding to my standards means setting boundaries with people, boundaries that they may not be used to. Even when it might be inconvenient. People have balked at my standards, in public and in private. I've also had to reconfigure some of my relationships in the process, and shit gets complicated as you recalibrate your relationships based on how people honor what you require, and vice versa. The relationship between my mama and me is probably one of the clearest examples of this.

My mama has always believed in a very authoritarian relationship between parent and child. I was raised in a household where things like passionate debate, differing opinions, or respectfully declining weren't options for me. If "I ain't one of your lil friends" were a person, it's my mama. Like most Black folks, I also grew up with corporal punishment. If any adult member of my family thought I was getting smart or acting up, it was nothing for them to pop me in my mouth or upside the head. If I did something egregious, or was fucking up in school, the belt would get involved. Accepting my punishment with as little resistance or defiance as possible was the only appropriate reaction. I was relieved to be going away to college because I naively thought it symbolized the end of this kind of control over my life. But it turned out my mama's stance on her parental role wasn't age restrictive. One day, when I was nineteen, we came to an impasse.

One of the milestones I achieved during my first year of college was getting a credit card. I didn't know shit about credit or how banks would ultimately benefit from my lack of experience or disposable income. What I knew is that if I was approved I would have an extra six hundred dollars at my disposal, and that it didn't require my mama's signature. But she knew I had it, and her only advice to me was to not be late on payments. Naturally, by the time I went home for spring break, the card was totally maxed out and I was being hit with penalty fees up the ass. But I felt very strongly about the fact that it was my responsibility and mine alone. I'd gotten myself into a mess, and for the first time, I didn't owe anyone an explanation for it. I was confident in my mistake because it was mine to make.

I was a couple days shy of returning to school when some

petty squabble between my mama and I led her to ask me about the credit card. It was actually more of a statement than a question. "I bet you maxed that card out, didn't you?" I admitted that I had. "Give it here," she demanded. I pretended like I didn't hear her and silently moved the card from my leather Dooney & Bourke wristlet into my back pocket, because I knew she'd try to take it. I felt firm in my position that the credit card was mine to keep. I would figure out a way to pay it down on my own, and I would certainly be keeping it with me. Still, I prayed, in vain, that she would just let it go. I sat on my bed and waited. "Gimme the card, Sesali!" she said again, standing in my doorway and staring me down. That's when I did something I'd never done before in my life. I told my mama, "No."

The word felt unnatural leaving my lips, as if it had never been part of my vocabulary before that moment. I didn't dare look at her as I said it. I waited for an explosion of anger. Instead she grabbed the wallet and began to go through it, looking for the credit card, not knowing that I'd already stashed it away. Standing over me, she demanded to know where it was. "I'm not going to give it to you." I was slightly emboldened since she hadn't knocked my head off when I first refused her. But my luck had just run out. She slapped me across the face with my own damn wallet.

Then I had another first. Rather than sit there passively while my mama went off, I tried to stand up and leave. I hadn't felt like I'd done anything wrong, and I for sure felt too old to still be getting physically pushed around by Mama for not doing every single thing she wanted me to do. I was over it. Unfortunately, she took the simple act of me raising my body off the bed as an indication that I wanted to "go toe-to-toe." I hadn't even made it completely upright before she pushed me back down and went on the offense. She swatted at my face, still hovering over me. Had she been pretty much anyone else, I would have started throwing punches. But despite the circumstances, I had enough reverence for my mother to never fight her like a bitch off the street. Still, I felt firmly that my days of being disciplined should have been over. So we tussled. *"Get the fuck off of me!"* I cursed at her as I tried to push her off. Neither of us had ever seen me like this. My brazen act of defiance shocked her. She stopped struggling, stood upright, and simply told me to get the fuck out of her house. I walked out barefoot and hurt, but oddly liberated.

Unfortunately, that was only the beginning of what has been an uphill battle in our relationship. My mama was nowhere near ready to interrogate what it meant to have an adult child and what changes that brought to our relationship. I shut down and resorted to keeping details about my life away from her, rather than risk her trying to exert power over me. This worked when I was over a hundred miles away at school and I spent most of my days posturing anyway. When I moved back in with her during my early twenties to finish my undergraduate degree at a different school, and finally started to get my shit together, our toxic dynamic bubbled right back to the surface. It was during these years that I was still building up my confidence, and with it came the awareness that our dynamic was emotionally draining and not healthy for my evolving sense of self. Before graduation, I had a job lined up, and I headed off to DC to start my life, relieved to have some space from her again.

During my visits back to Chicago, my mama and I would have some really intense arguments. She'd say or do something I didn't like, or perhaps it was me who offended her. She's a Virgo so she'd make her feelings about my perceived transgressions known, and then she'd expect that familiar unwavering silence from me in the face of her reprimands. She never hit me again, but she wanted my submission, and she interpreted my refusal to yield as combative disrespect, even when that wasn't my intention. It was extremely frustrating, and I began to resign myself to the fact that we'd just never have a good relationship. I was envious of women who had battled it out with their moms in their teen years, when puberty had sent their hormones flying, and then could count her among their best friends later in life. My mama vehemently rejected the idea of friendship between us because it implied we were peers and on equal footing. Meanwhile, I vehemently rejected the idea that anyone deserved my full subservience, not even the person who gave birth to me.

That's when I realized that I had to set a firm boundary in order to uphold my standards. We could apologize to each other and move past the specific arguments, but I knew our relationship wouldn't truly improve until I made it clear that my self-determination was more important to me than even my relationship with her. So I never backed down when I felt like she was being unreasonable, invading my privacy, or disregarding my boundaries. I had to hold my own line.

The standards I have for myself now involve respect. That means honoring my right to have emotions, different opinions, privacy, and the autonomy to make mistakes. For years my mama insisted that my smart mouth and refusal to show her respect were at the root of our issues. Now she can admit that she struggled with the fact that I was a grown ass woman and deserved to be treated as such. She's had to be more open and vulnerable, now that she can't rely on "Because I said so" to avoid a difficult, but more meaningful dialogue. I've also grown to appreciate her humanity and accept that just because we're different, that doesn't mean she won't support me. We couldn't have made it here, though, if I wasn't willing to risk our relationship in the service of my own needs.

Setting standards is figuring out the life you want to have. Maintaining standards is saying no to anything that isn't that. There are people who took up space in my life when my standards were different, and they had to see themselves out when they weren't up for the new ones. But my standards don't change, and that's on period. That's one of the things I've always loved about rap bitches. When they spit about what they deserve, what they want, and what they demand, there is no room for negotiation. Whether it's a refusal to have sex without first receiving the keys to a truck or a refusal to sign a contract if it doesn't guarantee ownership over their creative output, the spirit of female rap has always been about honoring the fundamental principles you set for your damn self. Today's female rap game has stepped it up because there is so much variety in style, aesthetic, content, and interests. Kamaiyah, the tomboy from the West Coast, exists right alongside Kash Doll, the former stripper from Detroit. They're in the same orbit as Doja Cat, who straddles a racialized fence between MC and pop princess, and exists right alongside Asian Doll, the Dallas rapper with a thing for guns. None of them shy away from what they like or why they like it; they just stand in what makes them comfortable.

That's what I encourage you to do. I'm not here to tell you what standards to set. I'm just telling you to have some and to hold to them.

Chapter 4

RUN ME MY MONEY

Can't argue with these lazy bitches.
I just raise my price.

—Megan Thee Stallion with Beyoncé, "Savage (Remix)"[1]

"You don't have a voice!" This is what my mama would say to me when I tried to express my displeasure about yet another decision she'd made for me, not considering my input. I was in high school and hadn't even gotten my first car yet. As a dependent, someone who relied on my mom's income and credit standing in order to have basic needs like housing, my opinions did not matter unless she cared to hear them, or they aligned with what she also wanted for me. What I thought? Irrelevant. Why? Because I was living in her house and she paid the fucking bills.

This is a fairly consistent principle throughout my family, and that of a lot of the other Black families I grew up around. There is a reason why asking your kid if they "got McDonald's money" is such a strong part of the Black parenting lexicon. It's a loaded question that not only references the literal cost of food in the US but also nods to the inherent power dynamics between people who have money and those who don't. Whether or not I would get the McDonald's meal I asked for was always up to chance, but I definitely felt deflated for having asked in the first place whenever my mama hit me with that line. It was an intimate reminder that nothing was in my control unless I could foot the bill for it. What was reinforced for me over and over again as a kid was that as long as other people had to open their wallets for me, I wasn't a fully realized person.

When people ask me what I was taught about money growing up, it's that

1. you need it; and
2. it's the key to autonomy, agency, and freedom.

In other words, you can't call any of your own shots, dictate your own schedule, or truly make your own decisions without the input of other people unless you can afford to do so.

I can imagine that the radical anticapitalists reading this are shook right now. They probably think I'm reinforcing materialism and unethical spending. And I know a lot of people are going to question the capitalist and consumerist themes that come up in this book as they relate to trap feminism. Let me tell you up front: I don't have any groundbreaking theories or solutions to global capitalism, the poverty that it has created for so many people around the world, or the inherent racism embedded within it. Sorry to disappoint, but I'm not an economist, and solving those kinds of problems are way above my pay grade. I don't have a single proposal around closing the gender gap between Black women and white men that doesn't involve running the latter's pockets. What I do know is that life is shitty for Black folks—*especially* for those of us who are femme, queer, nonbinary, differently abled, convicted of crimes, and noncitizens—when we are poor, and wouldn't you know it, we are the most likely to be broke.

If you've never been poor, let me inform you that being broke is the fucking worst. It makes a request for an eight-dollar meal from McDonald's a threat to your mama's weekly budget. It limits where you can go and what you can learn. It dictates how you look and how you get treated by other people. It both binds people together and puts a strain on those relationships. It decides whether or not you're going to have a doctor look into those pains you've been having in your stomach or you'll just keep self-medicating and hope for the best.

But it's not just shitty and stressful. Poverty literally kills people. Housing insecurity, lack of access to healthcare, and decent education have consequences that are bodily and generational. People are left to sit and rot in jail when they can't afford bail or don't have housing, keeping them away from their families. Not having access to quality education makes it harder to escape the cycle of poverty. When you cannot afford life-saving drugs or surgeries, you die.

When people say shit like "mOnEy DoEsN't BuY hApPiNeSs" or that being rich hasn't solved their problems or that finding ways to make money shouldn't be the most important thing in our personal lives or collective organizing efforts, they're speaking from a position of privilege that allows them to assume that being broke isn't absolutely terrible to the point of being inhumane. When looters made off on foot with mattresses and refrigerators in the midst of national protests following the murders of George Floyd, Breonna Taylor, and Tony McDade, it's because people in some communities can't afford to pay full price for mattresses and refrigerators. Not expensive jewelry. Not fancy cars. Basic humans needs like a bed to sleep on and an appliance to keep your food edible. This kind of financial scarcity is what most Black folks are running from. If it isn't already in bed with us and part of our day-to-day lives, it's right on our heels, threatening to bite us in the ass.

Black people, who are among those who have arguably gotten the shorter end of the capitalist stick, have always been judged the most harshly for their participation in it. Pathologizing poor Black folks for liking Jordans or for frivolously getting their nails done is easier than criticizing racist policies that support capitalism. So no, I don't have the same energy for a Black woman with $100,000 in student loans who paid $600 for a sew-in as I have for Jeff Bezos spending $65 million on a jet. And you shouldn't either. It took us hundreds of years to eradicate slavery, an economic system that relied on the free labor of enslaved Black people. You think our country's socially accepted focus on profit is going away in the foreseeable future? Nah. We sure as hell didn't create this system, and we don't want to suffer within it any more than we need to. So rather than hold our breaths waiting for equitable socialism to be adopted, we're out here trying to get paid.

But here's where shit got tricky for me: while my family insisted that having my own money was the key to my autonomy and self-sufficiency, they never really taught me *how* to be financially independent. Not only did I need to make my own money and be responsible with it; I also needed to figure out how to do all of it on my own. The only career advice I got from my granny was to "just get some teaching credentials," instead of trying to pursue a career that suited my interests and passions. Economic mobility is a bit of a myth in that it's often dangled in front of Black folks as the key to a better life, but without context, nuance, or a blueprint. From rappers to well-meaning grandparents, Black folks are told that there is treasure out there, just waiting for us to go get it. But we rarely get a map. So we end up stringing our paydays together in hopes that they'll eventually lead us to a promised land of prosperity or, at the very least, to being fully recognized as grown.

By the time I was fourteen, I was antsy to get a job. I was temporarily living with my granny in the suburbs. I was about to start high school, and I was already developing a taste for name-brand clothes, fresh Air Force 1s, and Coach purses. I was tired of having to grovel for money to join my homies at the skating rink, and I wanted to be able to buy dime bags of weed when I felt like it. I was also looking to the future: in a couple of short years I would be getting a driver's license and didn't want to have to rely on anyone else's budget in order for me to get behind the wheel.

Two of my best friends had gotten work permits to start working at the McDonald's in the next town over. You need a permit to work in Illinois if you're under sixteen, and the process of getting one often requires a parent's permission. I was so excited about the thought of making my own McDonald's money . . . at McDonald's, and I fully expected my granny to be on board. She'd gawked at the cost of my gym shoes, and whenever there was some expense I needed her to undertake, she'd exhale, "It's always something." I thought she would be happy to hear that I would be pulling some of my own weight. So I was frustrated and defeated when my granny instead responded with another classic Black parenting line: "Don't be in such a hurry to be grown." She wanted me to spend my freshman year of high school focused on being a good student. I would have to spend yet another year broke.

As an adult, I now can understand the position of privilege that both my granny and I were in at that time. She was able to take care of me so I could focus on stuff like school and hanging out with my friends. As long as I lived with her, I didn't have to divert my attention away from my studies to contribute to household expenses. That was more than I could say for some of my peers, and I should have been more grateful. Still, I wish the complete lack of control and subjugation that comes with being taken care of by someone else hadn't been made so explicit, and that there also had been some guidance on what exactly to do with money once I got some of it. But my granny was certainly right about one thing. I shouldn't have been in any hurry to start working. I would spend ten years working before I had a job that hit the trifecta I so deeply cherish now: I'm passionate about it, it pays enough for me to live the life I want to live, and it's legal.

A little over a year after that conversation with my granny, I was done with suburban life. You could say the streets were calling me. I wanted to get back to my other friends, the freedom of public transportation, and my mama. So I sat my granny down again and told her that I wanted to go back to living with my mother in the city. All she had to offer was a curt, "Fine. Go on, then." I wouldn't find this out until later, but my granny took it personal that I wanted to return to Chicago. She didn't understand how much the city meant to my personal identity. I had already seen and done too much in my fifteen years of life to feel 100 percent comfortable with how sterile the suburbs were. Only in hindsight can I see that what felt sterile was really safe, and to choose the streets over the suburbs was proof that I didn't yet understand what a privilege stability was.

I moved into my mama's one-bedroom apartment about halfway through my sophomore year of high school. She was just getting back on her feet after another bout with addiction and hadn't even lived there for a full year before I arrived. If we're being honest, she wasn't ready for me yet, but she also knew refusing to let me live with her after two years apart would break my heart. So we slept in the same bed, and I had to travel about forty-five minutes on the 59th Street bus and then another fifteen minutes on the Stony Island joint to get to school. Kenwood Academy isn't a ritzy private school by any stretch of the imagination, but it also wasn't your average CPS institution either. It sits smack dab in the middle of Hyde Park, the same neighborhood that shelters the prestigious University of Chicago from the rest of the South Side. Seriously, if you want to see what economic segregation in the US looks like, pick any street in Hyde Park and head south. Those nice campus buildings give way to something completely different when you get past 63rd Street. Wealthy professors and professionals in the area can send their teenagers to the university's private high school, Lab (short for Laboratory School), but Kenwood's close proximity to the university has helped it become more "cultured." There were opportunities for growth and expression that just didn't exist at Crete-Monee, my previous high school in the suburbs. And despite a majority of its students being Black, there was more economic diversity at Kenwood.

For teenagers, "economic diversity" means that there is a lot of pressure to keep up with the Joneses. Kenwood was known for being a bit of a fashion show, and it wasn't uncommon for junior and senior girls to carry their books in one hand and Louis Vuitton bags in the other. Guys rocked Coogi and Iceberg sweaters that cost nearly five hundred dollars a pop. One of my best guy friends drove a pearl-white Infiniti Q45 with rims and tinted windows (although to be fair, he'd pretty much dropped out by then). But even if you weren't at that level, you were expected to be able to at least rock a fresh Dooney & Bourke purse and keep up with the Jordan releases. The reputation that Kenwood has for being a site for style persisted throughout my early adulthood. Ask anyone you know from the South Side of Chicago about "Kenwood girls" and see what they say. Words like "bougie" and "stuck up" might come up if they're the hating type. But if they're honest, they know all the bad bitches went to Kenwood.

Needless to say, my desire to have a job grew more urgent by the day. Unlike my granny, my mama was more supportive of the idea. She actually helped me get my first job. Throughout my entire childhood she was the medical assistant to an ob-gyn whose practice was inside a clinic in Englewood. There was also a pediatrician, a family-practice doctor, a pharmacist, and a married dentist couple who operated out of the building. On the weekends, the dentists paid me under the table to help them and their secretary with billing, filing, and sterilizing their equipment. Summers were always busy at the clinic, when parents were trying to get their kids physicals, immunizations, and checkups before the school year started, so I worked there full-time during those months. Because I didn't have to deal with taxes, I was bringing home enough money to keep my nails done, get my hair done how I wanted it, and buy all the shitty takeout and junk food I wanted. And yes, I bought myself a Coach purse, too.

Once that job ended in the fall, I was used to having a certain amount of money in my pocket. So the hunt for a replacement was on. Plus, I was ready to go "legit." Most of my friends were starting to get jobs in food service, and a handful of them worked at Potbelly Sandwich Shops across the city. But I had my eyes on retail. In my teenage mind that seemed more "upscale" than making sandwiches and soups. My first legit job was a holiday seasonal position in the juniors section at Nordstrom on Michigan Avenue. (Yep, the same place where I would be arrested three years later.)

Nordstrom sits on Chicago's Magnificent Mile, which is a tourist trap that also hosts department stores like Neiman Marcus and luxury boutiques the likes of Cartier and Chanel. The three months I worked at Nordstrom was its own case study in privilege. Nordstrom is where I mastered my "white voice." Most of my customers there were tourists or Chicagoans from other parts of the city who were enjoying a weekend of shopping downtown. But almost all of them were at least middle class and not from my part of town, so I had to adapt. It was an easy job in which I spent most of the day keeping our section tidy and clean, helping customers find stuff, and ringing them up at the register. Because I was working in the juniors section, which targeted younger shoppers, I didn't experience all of the snobbery some of my coworkers in other departments told me about from their wealthy customers. Most of the people I had to interact with were young women just enjoying their excursions and excited to go to the next store.

But there was one girl who would come in alone, even though I could tell she wasn't much older than me. She stood out because she was a Black girl with natural sandy-red hair and freckles. She'd use a credit card that had a man's name on it, I'm assuming her dad's, and she had a "white voice" that was way more natural than mine. I knew she came from a well-off family. She was short, and she often wanted her items sent down to our in-house tailors for alterations. She'd toss a heap of clothes in front of me and rattle off what she wanted sent downstairs and what she wanted done to it, without an ounce of friendliness in her tone. I knew that Nordstrom offered alteration services, but I rarely got any of those orders, and certainly not for a fucking pair of jeans. It seemed petty and unnecessary to me, and her nasty tone made it worse. At sixteen, I didn't know that what I was experiencing was entitlement, the specific kind that comes from being in high school and not being at all excited about having a pair of jeans that cost over $150. I'd gotten this job because I wanted to make enough money to keep up with the Joneses. But here was one of them right in front of me, and she was an asshole. I was slowly learning that being rich was less about what you have than *who* you are. I realized that no amount of purses could suddenly make me part of her world.

My next job offered up a completely different customer-relations experience. Working at fancy ass Nordstrom made me a shoo-in for a position in the shoe department at JCPenney in Ford City Mall. We served mostly Black and Mexican American working-class families on Chicago's Southwest Side. I actually ended up making more money there because I made a commission in addition to my hourly wages. I made my first check over $1,500 after Easter, when parents bought dress shoes in bulk for church services and family gatherings (which was great because by then I'd gotten a car and was responsible for gas and insurance). When it was slow at Penney's, I would fool around with one of my coworkers in the back room where we kept our overstock while he snorted cocaine off a key. I found out later that his baby mama worked in another department.

I hated working at JCPenney because the management treated their employees like shit, probably because many of us were Black and Mexican American working-class people, just like the customers who were making sure their pockets were lined. They didn't respect us and watched us intently as if we would make off with their merchandise at any moment. On my last shift before I went away to college, the assistant manager was doing a walk-through of the store before closing and made a comment about me not working hard enough. I responded with some smart remark, and he asked for my name to start the process of getting me fired. I told him it was my last day anyway and that I didn't give a shit. He said, "Well, I'll make sure you never work at another one of our stores," and I responded, "Gladly." To this day, I've never shopped at JCPenney because of the sour taste it left in my mouth. Nordstrom taught me how the privileged spend their money; JCPenney taught me how terrible it is to work for them.

Then I started college. Like many students, part of my financial-aid package included a work-study program. These weren't memorable or fulfilling jobs. Freshman year I endlessly filed away applications in the admissions office and tutored local middle schoolers as part of the America Reads program. I didn't have to physically clock in and out, so just like my classes, showing up was a huge challenge for me. To be honest, I'm still kind of like that: if you want me to do something that

I don't want to do, you're going to have to make me. Needless to say, I'm glad I was housed in the dorms and not responsible for any major bills yet, because I was constantly missing work.

I was hired at Borders in Chicago over the summer after my freshman year, the same summer I got arrested. It marked my reluctant return to retail, but it was a job I was actually excited about. I've always loved to read, and Borders would let employees essentially treat the inventory like a library. You could check out books and return them with ease. Plus, we got press copies of books that we could keep for free. I would show up to shifts early just to spend some time chilling in the café and reading. As I mentioned, when I was in jail, I just called out of work and switched shifts with one of my coworkers. I returned a few days later like nothing had happened and never told them that I had been arrested. I kept my job, and they didn't even have to run a background check when I transferred to the Champaign, Illinois, location when school resumed in the fall. I worked at Borders for nearly two years, through my sophomore and junior years of college, during a time when they continued to see declining sales thanks to the rising popularity of Amazon.

Moving from one of Illinois's busiest stores to one off campus in a rural college town meant that I took a pay cut. But it's not like I was on a promotion track there anyway. Yes, I liked working at Borders, but I was also becoming more and more aware that none of these little part-time gigs would matter in the grand scheme of my life. I'm not saying this was the right attitude to have—especially not when I was broke and had a criminal record—but I also wasn't exactly wrong. Still, I had to start hustling if I was going to make it.

My first stab at a side gig came when I tried to be a Pure Romance consultant, or, in other words, a freelance seller of sex toys and lubes. Pure Romance is just like every other pyramid scheme, except it's not a scheme. Consultants are responsible for finding customers who are interested in hosting private toy parties, where you show and sell the products. It's a raging good time for girls who giggle at the sight of butt plugs and middle-aged women who've had a few cocktails. Consultants are responsible for maintaining their own inventory and constantly seeking out new customers. Really good consultants make even more money by convincing other women that they, too, can experience financial freedom as Pure Romance consultants, and pocket a percentage of their recruit's sales.

Unfortunately, I had no clue how to market myself and was too lazy to figure it out at the time. It took me over a month to ship my first and last customers their dildos. This did not stop me from putting Pure Romance on my résumé to get a job at not one but two local sex shops near campus in the years that followed. One of them had a "theater" downstairs where men could watch porn and, naturally, leave semen all over the floor. Let it be known that my retail experience is vast and disgusting, and most times, I wasn't paid enough to put up with the bullshit I had to deal with.

One of my more lucrative side hustles was writing papers for other students. I've always been good at writing, a skill some of my friends in STEM majors did not share. I got my first "client" when a friend came to me in desperation. He had a four-page paper due, and the thought of writing it was clearly stressing him out; he half-jokingly offered me fifty bucks to do it for him. I really needed the money so I told him I would. Plus, a four-page paper wasn't shit to me. I researched and wrote it in a couple of hours. I didn't expect this to become a regular gig, but after he got a good grade and told some of his friends about it, the requests started rolling in weekly. The money was even easier, and safer, when my clientele expanded to the local community college, where the courses weren't as rigorous. Writing papers was a great way to supplement what little I was making at Borders. Looking back, I should have charged more. After I returned from a summer internship in 2009, Borders didn't have the budget to rehire me. I was completely assed out, and writing papers for other people wouldn't cover all of my bills, especially now that I had Sandy.

*   *   *

I had spent my entire freshman year, and part of sophomore year, without a car. The '97 Dodge Stratus I'd had in high school didn't make it a year under my poor upkeep and overuse. I had to rely on friends or public transportation to get me where I needed to go, including the two-hour drive north to Chicago if no one from my family felt like driving to get me. I remember wanting a Monte Carlo, but my mama insisted on me having something more reliable since I would be driving on the interstate and in snow.

My mama and I were at one of the many shabby used-car dealerships on Western Avenue. People from Chicago know that the dealerships on Western specialize in getting people with shitty credit approved for shitty loans to drive away with one of their shitty used cars. Sandy was different, though. She was the baddest bitch on the lot, and I thought she was out of my league. I would have been happy to drive off in an older or different model. But the salesman talked her up. She was nearly new and came with features like heated leather seats and a sound system that put some custom kits to shame. My mama was also enticed by the idea of a newer car for me because I would be driving two hours on the interstate, each way, when traveling from college to home.

I'd saved a chunk of my student refund check to cover most of the down payment but would need a cosigner since I didn't have a full-time job or much of a credit history. I knew that I could hustle up only about $250 a month for a note. The best the salesman could do for us in order to drive off with Sandy was a hefty note of nearly $400 a month. My mama covered the rest of the down payment and agreed to take on the remaining $150 a month. We signed the paperwork, and I drove Sandy off the lot. We'd successfully gotten a car for me!

And it nearly ruined our relationship.

Neither one of us could really afford Sandy. That's the bottom line. My mama had been an LPN for only two years at that time and was solidly working-class. There were months when she didn't pay her portion and I had to eat the entire bill. As I've already explained, I was pretty irresponsible when I was in college, which is why it took me six years to graduate. There was also my weed habit, the stealing phase that landed me in jail, and the fact that I was working at a book retailer that was in the process of shutting down for good. So there were a couple of years when I couldn't always pay my portion either. I racked up accidents, repairs, and tickets in Chicago faster than I could pay them. Several times my mama had to shell out more than she'd budgeted for so that her credit didn't suffer along with mine.

This became leverage for her in our relationship. If she was upset with me, she'd threaten to take Sandy away, like I was sixteen and it was a PlayStation. I couldn't have a single dissenting opinion or take the wrong tone without being reminded of *all* the money she was paying for *my* car. The politics of our relationship aside, the tension between us during the six years we were paying for Sandy is a perfect example of how money, and not quite having enough of it, can put a lot of pressure on a relationship.

Stepping back and looking at the bigger picture, my mama and I were both trying to dig ourselves out of messes we'd made for each other. Her bounce back had been a long time coming, so I understand how desperately she wanted a responsible daughter who could lessen her burdens instead of adding more to her plate. I desperately wanted a mother who could just afford to buy me a car outright so that I, too, could have one less thing to worry about. Unfortunately, neither of us could be what the other person wanted.

The obvious solution is that I should have purchased a

cheaper car. It would have saved us both so much money and stress. I can't help but imagine how different our relationship would have been if either of us had had the financial sense or autonomy to make that decision at the time. Or how different things could have been if, at the very least, either of us had had an extra $10,000 lying around. We stretched ourselves way too thin just so I could have a car that wouldn't leave me stranded on the side of the road in rural America.

*   *   *

Over the course of what should have been my last semester of college, my electricity was cut off, Sandy was at risk of being repossessed, and an eviction process was started on the studio apartment I was renting. During those five months, I strung money together by working as a nanny part-time and hustling full-time. I wrote papers here and there; I filed a renter's insurance claim for a "break in" that took place at my apartment; and I did sex work (more on that later). Because I'd lost my financial aid, I wasn't enrolled in classes and hadn't figured out what I was going to do next. I didn't tell any of my family what was going on because I was ashamed and dreading their reaction. The weight of my circumstances sent me into a depression that I only made worse by getting high and binge eating. At one point I burned my lip on a blunt and the blister that formed didn't go away for months. It was a physical manifestation of the desolation I was living in.

Defeated, I reluctantly moved back home. I was ready to start over. In the next two years, I returned to school and worked an assortment of shitty jobs that didn't really pay enough. I found a customer-service job at a nondescript office in Northbrook, a suburb about forty-five minutes away from the South Side. My job was to cold-call folks all day to get them to "interview" for a job. The job? Selling Vector knives. I was fired after a few months because I wasn't hitting my numbers. (Feel free to laugh. It's funny.) Then someone told me about a call center called Telesight that was hiring without background checks. I didn't have to cold-call anyone; instead, we conducted customer-satisfaction surveys for companies like Home Depot. The job was downtown, which was convenient to campus, and across the street from Open Books, one of my favorite used bookstores. But I worked long shifts in a highly controlled environment. I couldn't have anything in my cubicle except one of the word-find puzzles they passed out during the shift, and only if I asked for it. I stuck with the job for as long as I could, but it was truly mind-mushing work. One day I snapped. I just couldn't bring myself to show up. I didn't bother to call in, and they never called me. It was my first "Fuck that job" moment. I don't regret it either.

Throughout the two years after I moved home, I was rebuilding, but my big picture hadn't changed. I knew that I needed to get my degree if I wanted to make more than eleven dollars an hour and experience the independence I still hadn't nailed. I was willing to take risks because I never again wanted to have to push my car to the gas station only to put five dollars in the tank. I didn't want to ever feel like I couldn't hold people in my life accountable or move the way I wanted to because I needed someone else to pay my bills.

Moving to DC in 2012 was an intentional decision. I'd fallen in love with the city during my internship at a reproductive justice nonprofit three years before. While I was there, I'd also built a network of friends in the progressive nonprofit space, which I wanted to work in. I had gotten a job offer from the United States Student Association, which supported student governments in organizing their student bodies around progressive issues. I became the training director and was responsible for selecting and overseeing our two organizing cohorts, including their training weekends, and planning our two major conferences. At a bigger organization with a larger budget, this would have been a lofty job for a bitch fresh out of undergrad. It also would have paid more. I was good at my job once I figured out how the bureaucracy worked, but my salary was only $34,000. I got a $2,000 raise after a nasty contract negotiation with the union. It was the most money I'd ever made, but it damn sure wasn't enough.

A couple of months before my contract was up, I was poached by Planned Parenthood Action Fund, their national policy headquarters, for a tragic $42,000 to be their national campus organizer. Turns out that while I can coordinate the fuck out of some conference logistics, plan an amazing party, and keep a crowd engaged, I'm actually not a great political organizer. Perhaps I would have been more incentivized to learn if

I wasn't trying to pay rent, a car note, and student loans while living in DC on less than $45,000 a year.

I hated every minute of working at Planned Parenthood, from the untenable pace to the racial microaggressions of the white feminists who worked there. For the first time in my life I had anxiety attacks that would keep me awake for hours. After I went on a particularly bad work trip to West Virginia that left me feeling completely incompetent and demoralized, I started plotting my exit. I knew that if I didn't leave I would probably be fired anyway. I started looking at grad school options before I flew back to DC and found a partially funded gender studies program that was still accepting applications. I had three days to turn everything in, and I submitted it from the SuperShuttle on my way back to my apartment. After two more months of agony, I got accepted into Georgia State in March. The program didn't start until August, but I submitted my two-week resignation letter anyway.

The next few months were a struggle for a lot of different reasons (some of which will be discussed later). I got a temp job at a law firm for a few weeks, then I took on a short-term administrative project for my former boss and friend. I also hustled a little bit on the side (I was still moonlighting as a sex worker) and had a compassionate landlord who put my security deposit toward my last month's rent. I road-tripped to Chicago in July (the morning after I went to Beyoncé and Jay-Z's On the Run Tour, thanks to the charity of a friend) to spend my last month as a bum bitch before heading to Atlanta for grad school. I borrowed $150 from my mama to cover gas for the trip, because I'd spent the last bit of coin in my bank account paying my car note for the month. When I got there my family didn't let me hear the end of it. My aunt was particularly opinionated about it. "Why would you quit your job without having another one lined up?" she wanted to know. I knew she wouldn't understand my reasoning, so I tried to get her off of my case by admitting that I just didn't want to talk about it. She reminded me that I had to do some talking when I was the one who needed to borrow money to get home.

It was degrading and humiliating, for sure. I had been proud of the two years I'd spent figuring things out on my own with the little bit of money I was making, and now here I was, starting again. And my aunt wasn't wrong about how financially irresponsible it was to quit my job before I had something else lined up to hold me over for a few months. The difference this time was that I had a clear path forward. Grad school was starting, even if I showed up there with only the clothes on my back. I didn't regret leaving my job, but I did vow not to put myself in that position again. Being broke was debilitating to my mental health. It made me feel cut off from the rest of the world and made it extremely hard to connect with my family. I fall into despondence quickly, and it becomes crippling. This is why I, and so many other people, find trap music particularly inspiring.

If you've ever wondered why getting money is such an important part of trap culture, it's because too many of us have lived with this feeling of hopelessness and despair. Money is emotional for us. My theory is that designer clothes and foreign cars are less about our proximity to wealth and more about our creating distance between us and the severe struggle of being broke—or at the very least these things offer some relief from it. That's what separates trap music from Jay-Z's one percent vibe. What trap culture lacks in ideas for overthrowing the economic structure that crushes so many of its own, it makes up for in creative reprieves. Paying $500 for a bottle of liquor at a club is such a drastically different experience from waiting three days for a paycheck to get the lights turned back on. The back of a Bentley *feels* way different from any seat on the bus.

While I heard my family loud and clear when they insisted that I could only experience freedom when I was financially independent, I also watched how they defined their own "success." They allowed themselves to experience small hits of that feeling we're all chasing: whatever satisfaction and rest is waiting on the other side of "making it." For my aunt Michelle, it's diamonds. "I need to stay out of Albert's [the jeweler]" is a regular quip of hers. For my granny, it's housewares and home decor. Unlike my friends whose grandparents' homes have looked exactly the same since they were born, I'm old enough to remember at least two major remodels and countless furniture overhauls. Granny has made a home that she can appreciate. For my sister, it's the excitement of a new designer bag and fresh bundles of virgin hair. We're alike in that way.

When I moved to Atlanta, I used my stipend and some student loans to take care of debt. I got a weekend gig as a cocktail waitress at a Jamaican nightclub to take care of my discretionary spending. My shit was finally "together" in a way that it hadn't been before, and it helped make Atlanta two of the best years my adulthood has seen.

During my last few months there, I saved up enough money to fund my move when I got my first writing job in New York. It's been five years on the East Coast with a career in media. I haven't had to ask my family for money once.

It's my job to keep it that way, and I find comfort in that. It's a personal challenge I'll rise to every time. I no longer entertain relationships, jobs, or experiences that threaten my livelihood. I know personal responsibility is a tricky topic in the context of capitalism and how it affects marginalized communities. I'm certainly not trying to tell anybody to lean in. But I had to understand the situation I was in, the system that had created it, *and* the choices I had made under those circumstances. The truth is that at various times in my life I was both broke and irresponsible. I needed to get my shit together. When I did, so much changed. My mama and I can work on being loving and supportive of each other now that our finances are no longer entangled. I can afford to adorn and celebrate my body in different ways, whether it be a fresh sew-in or a new set of nails. Most important, on more nights than not, I get to rest without the fear that I can't afford the roof over my head. So yes, I'm all about my fucking coin, and I need you to run me my money.

Chapter 5

PLAN B

I feel like being, like, sexual and shit, like, I don't see nothing wrong with that.

—Sukihana[1]

I'll be the first to acknowledge that Black girls are hypersexualized. Our bodies are heavily surveilled and our behaviors unfairly policed out of fear that we will misuse our sexuality. Any expression of autonomous sexual expression from a Black girl often falls into the prohibited category. What we wear, how we walk, and where we go are all regulated in service of repressing our sexuality. Even our dances scream danger to untrained eyes. We're expected to protect ourselves from abusers, and it's us who are held accountable when we are abused. People get on the internet and call Black babies who can barely speak "thotlers" because of how their little bodies are bent in a photo or how an adult dresses them. We're denied the right to innocence before we're old enough to know what it means. It's a fucked-up prerequisite to the misogynoir we will have to face for most of our lives. In some cases, this early hypersexualization will be used to justify misogynoir

Things That Can Get a Black Girl Labeled "Fast"

- Developing breasts or hips too soon

- Having friends of another gender

- Having an interest in makeup or fashion

- Dancing

- Walking a certain way

- Enjoying contemporary music

- Being sexually victimized

- Researching sexual health

- Having a crush

- Breaking any of your parents' rules

and other sinister forms of harm. The line between being called "fast" (a term typically reserved for girl children when someone else projects premature sexuality onto them) and being called a "thot" is extremely thin.

With that being said, anyone who called me fast when I was younger was on the money. I've been fascinated with sexuality, or at least super curious about it, ever since I was young. I played "house"—the game where you pretend to be a couple at the head of a household, thus giving you and your play partner permission to do stuff like kiss and dry hump—with boys *and* girls. I was thrilled to get my period when I was ten because I thought it would suddenly unlock some of the mystery that sexuality was always shrouded in. My first tongue kiss was around that age, in a photo booth at Odyssey Fun World. My "boyfriend" gave me a toy ring that I wouldn't take off until it turned my finger green weeks later. I loved catching the explicit versions of songs in someone's car or house (one of my favorites was Akinyele's "Put It in Your Mouth"), and I reveled in how grown up knowing the words made me feel. I remember my god-siblings and I discovering *Real Sex* through TV static because HBO wasn't part of our cable package. We'd crane our necks and squint, trying to catch a glimpse of a titty or two bodies in action. As DVDs became more and more popular, one of my simple joys was coming across an unmarked disc in someone's home, popping it into the DVD player, and discovering that it was a bootlegged porno. I often found the ridiculous titles (I kid you not, one of them was a volume in a series of films called Tastes Like Tuna) and the bad acting off-putting, even at that age. But I would tolerate both for the opportunity to secretly watch people fuck.

Despite so many attempts to steer me in the opposite direction—by the adults in my life and a culture that had divested from the idea of Black girls having a healthy relationship with sex—I was drawn to the palpable energy around sex. I realized that the essence of sex wasn't limited to physical contact between bodies. It was a whole vibe, and I wanted to catch the wave. I also understood very early on that there were outcomes of sex that extended beyond the act itself, and they weren't always good. While I had to keep my preoccupation with sexual energy a secret, I was exposed to those "outcomes" in a very direct way.

As I mentioned before, my mother manned the front desk for an ob-gyn. We'll call him Dr. J, and he employed my mama from the time I was about two years old until I was sixteen or seventeen. The clinic was in Englewood, Chicago's "murder capital" and one of the neighborhoods with the city's highest rates of poverty. The neighborhood also became my stomping grounds in the summers, when I went to work with my mama because she wasn't trying to spare the extra money for child-care or camp.

Rarely can a doctor's office be described as pleasant, but clinics built to serve a community of poor people are particularly bleak. When Dr. J's office had been housed at Reymar Clinic, the dimly lit hallways were paneled with dark wood, and dirty-looking linoleum covered the floors. The mix of medical equipment and supplies made it smell sour, like rubber gloves and old mop water. Knowing what I know now, it could have easily doubled as a BDSM dungeon. But that didn't stop me from roaming the halls, popping into the offices of the different doctors to chat with their secretaries and snoop around. The illustrated renderings of human insides and skeleton models made me feel like I had free access to my own personal museum every day. Dr. J's office was a little brighter, with a lighter finish on the wood and a row of connected orange chairs for patients to wait on, but it wasn't much more inviting than the rest of the place. At some point most of the doctors migrated from Reymar to an updated building called Mall Medical Center, where the builders had had the decency to paint the walls white and install fluorescent lighting. It was bad enough folks had to sit in the clinic, sometimes for hours; they should at least not be made to feel like they were underground.

Organized on a wooden display case in Dr. J's waiting room were pamphlets and brochures with information on topics like birth control, breastfeeding, intimate-partner violence, and sexually transmitted diseases. I would read through all of them. What I didn't understand on a page, I'd figure out later via context clues and overheard conversations between the people coming in and out of the office on a daily basis. See, the clinic (and specifically Dr. J's office) was a communal hub, not unlike a beauty shop. Women would come for a checkup and leave having found a loophole to get their kids into a better school or more WIC benefits (essentially food stamps for moms and kids), a new girl to do their hair, or more details on a lawyer who could represent their family member in a court case. (Yes, the defense attorney for my shoplifting case was referred to my mama by a patient-friend whose husband was a big-time drug dealer.)

But sometimes the reason for the doctor visit was fascinating in itself. I once witnessed a fourteen-year-old, and her mother, discover that she was pregnant. Neither of them had been expecting it. The shock, fear, embarrassment, anger, and disappointment radiated off them and into the entire office. It was a heartbreaking scene. But I also saw plenty of women bop out of the office with a pep in their step because their pregnancy test had come back negative. One time a chick came to see Dr. J because she was experiencing pain after having sex with a new partner. Apparently the guy's dick was so big that he'd caused minor tissue damage inside her. She got a good laugh out of sharing that with her friend, even though her pussy was sore. I saw the hopelessness of women stuck in abusive relationships, wincing every time they moved with bruised ribs or cut faces. Want to know why I'm vigilant about changing my tampon in a timely manner? Because I'm haunted by the awful smell that would fill the small office whenever Dr. J had to retrieve one that had been abandoned inside some poor girl's coochie for too long.

While women waited for Dr. J, they talked. I heard stories of partners cheating with other people, sending their girlfriends into Dr. J's office for STI screenings. I heard the stories of women who weren't sure who had fathered their unborn children (and my mama's hilarious advice to just pick the most qualified candidate). Women who didn't have insurance would buy sample packs of birth control from my mama for twenty dollars a pop, and I would ride shotgun with her as she dropped them off all over the South Side.

Thousands of women came to Dr. J's office with problems, and most of the time they left with some sort of solution. Those women loved him, and my mama, for that. The two of them were hood heroes. The side of one of their tall file cabinets was covered with photographs collected over the years. Patients would bring in pictures of kids my mama and her boss had helped bring into the world. There were pictures of the patients themselves going to prom or visiting their boyfriends in jail, the boyfriends we'd hear so much about but never meet. It wasn't uncommon for girls to show up for their doctor visit and recognize other folks they knew on the picture wall. Girls they'd fought, their baby daddy's other kids, or their second and third cousins. My first love, whom I hadn't seen or heard from in over a year, when accompanying one of his sisters to a doctor visit, saw my picture on the wall and immediately used the office phone to call me. When my mama hired her best friend to replace her, she kept the picture wall intact and growing. The pictures spanned years and told the story of generations of Black women in Englewood.

My time at Mall Medical Center helped me understand that

if I was going to be sexually active, I needed to be informed. I needed to know what services were available to me and how to access them, how to prepare and protect myself, how to plan for the outcomes I did and didn't want, and how to advocate for myself. I also understood the power of community in supporting one another, so I offered myself up as a resource for my network of friends who were, one by one, starting their own journeys with sex. All of us were trying to keep our sex lives hidden from our parents. I became the go-to person when my friends had questions about what was happening with their bodies or needed stuff like condoms or birth control. When we were in high school, one of my best friends (we were introduced as little kids because her mother was a patient of Dr. J's) found out she was pregnant after I administered a test that I'd swiped from my mama's desk. It was also me who talked her through the process of getting an abortion when she made it clear she wasn't ready for a baby. I enjoyed playing that role as an advocate. For a long time I thought being a gynecologist would allow me to do it full-time. As I'll explain later, I was way off base.

Either way, though, the arsenal of information I gathered up from spending months in Dr. J's office made me feel empowered and emboldened. I was eager to put it to use. I lost my virginity when I was twelve years old. (For the record: "virginity" is a heteronormative, cisnormative social construct. It only acknowledges a penis penetrating a vagina as sex and implies that something has been "lost" after this interaction. But I didn't know any of this at twelve, so for the purposes of this story, I'm going to reference virginity. It's nostalgic. Feel free to cancel me.) I'll never forget the date, December 27, 2000, because it's also my homegirl's birthday, and every year for twenty years I've reminded her. She hates it, but it's tradition now.

Here's what happened: My mama's new boyfriend had a daughter who was around my age—let's call her Tyran. We became pretty close. For example, one time we caught her father with another woman in my mama's car and we confronted them both as a united front. Under the banner of sisterhood, we threatened to whoop her ass, together. Tyran would spend weekends at my apartment, where her father lived with my mama and me. But I preferred to stay at her mom's place in Englewood. Tyran's siblings didn't really like me, and her mother was kind of mean, but I gladly tolerated all of it because I had other motives. I was twelve and full-on boy crazy . . . and there were a *lot* of boys in Tyran's neighborhood. One house in particular, right across the alley from hers, was full of them. Five brothers, aged nine, eleven, twelve, fourteen, and sixteen, lived there together, and their thirteen-year-old cousin, Jerron, also spent a lot of time there. The six of them would congregate on their back porch, in view of Tyran's place.

With the exception of the younger two, they were just as enthusiastic about sex as I was, especially Jerron. He was tall and skinny, with small, beady eyes and full lips. The only thing he liked more than basketball was the pursuit of girls. I was infatuated with him. By the time I met him, he'd already fooled around with Tyran and a couple of other girls in the neighborhood. As I met more and more of the kids around Tyran's house, I realized that I was actually the only "virgin." But not for much longer. The sexual energy amongst the group of teenagers in such close proximity was frenzied, like sharks circling in bloodied waters. I kept myself right in the middle of it, knowing that my time was coming.

Jerron and I had sex on the floor of his cousins' shared room while they were distracted. (Romantic, I know.) We hadn't planned it. It was too cold to be outside, so I joined him and a couple of his cousins in the bedroom they shared. It was already dark, and one of them put a porno on the TV. I acted indignant about it, as if the whole thing was immature and beneath me. As high as I was on nervous anticipation, I couldn't let any of that show. Jerron invited me to join him on the floor because his cousins were occupying the bunk beds, engrossed in their film. Jerron and I cuddled up underneath a sheet for "privacy" while my heart started to race.

I refused to initiate anything and followed his lead, which was really just a sequence of requests made through kisses on my neck and lips. "Come here." "Lie down." "Take these off." My only assertive remark came after he was on top of me, both of us still in our underwear, though. When he started to slide my panties to the side, I asked, "Do you have a condom?" He did. Knowing what was about to happen, I opened my legs a little more for him, and boom. I was officially not a virgin anymore. It didn't hurt like so many girls made me think it would. That could have been because I'd already been masturbating for years, or the fact that Jerron only had a thirteen-year-old dick. But it also didn't feel great, which is what I expect from sex as an adult, and I have more clarity on why that is now.

Sure, I was excited about sexuality, informed about the potential outcomes, and knew how to prevent the bad ones. But at twelve, I didn't have a politic around pleasure. I wanted to have sex for every reason *except* that I wanted to cum. Something that has always stuck with me about that first time with Jerron was how I kept resting my hand on the wooden frame of the bunk beds towering over us, instead of on his body. At one point Jerron physically took my arm and wrapped it around his back. He liked it there, and he wasn't ashamed of that. As excited as I was to be penetrated, I was terrified of the intimacy that came along with it. It felt unnatural to be vulnerable about what I liked and didn't like. I didn't have deep feelings for Jerron as much as I just enjoyed the thrill of his attention. I would love him, eventually, but that would come later. So would my understanding of what I even liked sexually. All I knew then was that what I had experienced on that floor was certainly not my idea of pleasure.

The only thing scarier to society than a Black girl having sex is the idea that she might be facilitating that sex on her own terms and liking it. Attempts to kill Black girls' sexuality are meant to work proactively, from the inside out. The first casualty of this rhetoric is the very idea of pleasure itself. Denial, surveillance, threats, and shame are all imposed on us to create a process of self-regulation and discipline. So the joys of intimacy and passion are kept secret, and many of us develop our first crushes and experience our first kisses under a blanket of shame. Black girls don't get the birds and the bees talk, at least none of the ones I know did. We get "I better not catch you messin' around with none of these lil boys!" "Don't come up in here pregnant!" or "Ain't no fuckin' in my house." Occasionally, a curious family member might notice a widening of the hips or a change in the way you walk into a room and ask, "You fuckin' yet?" but it's a huge risk to admit it if you are.

All of this conditioning is meant to get Black girls to a place where they just "know better" when it comes to sex. We're supposed to be aware that sex is an option, a temptation (or threat) swirling around us at all times. But we're supposed to *know better* than to act on it or even talk about it. If we discover that it feels really good to have certain parts of our bodies touched or stimulated, we're supposed to *know better* than to take advantage of that sensation. All this conditioning really does is keep us isolated. Navigating desire and sex becomes a solo journey that we have to explore without the support of our families, churches, or schools. The consequences of this isolation are grave.

Silencing the sexuality of Black girls is dangerous because unlike pregnancy and sexually transmitted diseases—the "shameful" outcomes that will likely reveal themselves even if we try to ignore them—predators can use this silence to their advantage. It protects them while making Black girls easier prey. If Black girls are conditioned to keep our sex lives a secret, if we expect punishment from the authority figures in our lives who become privy to our sexual activity, if we're denied a full understanding of power and consent as they relate to sex, then how can we identify, let alone avoid, the people who would seek to take advantage of us? These mixed messages are how I ended up, at thirteen, in an ongoing sexual relationship with one of my neighbors and didn't think there was anything wrong with the fact that he was in his twenties.

When this neighbor was suddenly interested in private, one-on-one conversations with me when our block was quiet, I didn't distinguish him from any of the other boys and men I wasn't supposed to be talking to. I didn't distinguish what we did together from any of my other teenage infractions, like smoking weed. I thought I was grown and considered the attention of an older guy to be a welcome challenge. A burgeoning car booty, I loved how mature I felt when he would pick me up and drop me off. I didn't mind walking the extra block or two so no one from our block would actually see us together, something we had both agreed on because I knew I'd be in trouble for being in a car with a boy. Like during the sexual experience I'd had with a boy my own age, I made sure my neighbor and I used condoms every time. I gossiped on the phone with my friends about the sexual acts and positions I was experiencing for the first time with him.

My understanding of sexual predators was limited to urban legends and rumors of prepubescent kids being mistreated by pedophiles. We called them Chesters, short for Chester the

car booty:

A slang term for girls, usually teenagers, who are easily wooed by niggas who don't have to catch the bus or train because they have a car.

Molester, a fictional, rhyming name that only pushed them further into mythological territory. Images of other people's creepy uncles in the basement, drunks lurking in alleyways, or weird older men who drove vans dominated my imagination. Yes, the idea of them was scary, but I didn't anticipate running into them in the hood and knew to avoid them if I did. Even the stories I'd heard through the grapevine about girls my age and older being sexually assaulted were brutal tales of them being held at gunpoint or gang-raped after being outnumbered. They'd said no or tried to get away and their attackers didn't care. The common thread in all of this was the only defining characteristic of a sexual predator that was offered to me: he had to be someone I didn't *want* to have sex with. This wasn't the case for me, or any of the other girls I knew who were hopping in and out of cars with grown men.

The myth of the "perfect victim" hurts all survivors of sexual assault, harassment, or coercion, but it really does hit different for Black girls. For many people, my indifference toward the age gap between my neighbor and I, my excitement about having an older boo, and my "fastness" meant that my neighbor's actions were justified. Had the block found out that I was creeping around with him, the worst that probably would have happened was we'd be the topic of some juicy conversations. It would have been on par with finding out that so-and-so's daughter was pregnant by her sister's baby daddy. My motives and behaviors would have likely been called into question and condemned. But I don't think anyone would have called for my neighbor's arrest or any other form of accountability. Because what I know for sure is that we don't have the same energy for grown men who want to fuck minors that we do for underage Black girls who didn't do everything in their power to make themselves unattractive and unavailable to those men.

In 2013, in response to a viral hashtag about how being "fast" or "fast-tailed" is often weaponized against Black girls, I wrote about this experience with my neighbor. The backlash, mostly from other Black women, was swift. They accused me of invalidating the experiences of Black girls who are hypersexualized and unprotected. Someone suggested that I had Stockholm syndrome because I had positioned myself as a consenting party. They thought my narrative and the assertion that *I* had wanted it were meant to derail the very important conversation about those who did not. None of this was true. What I was trying to say, and admittedly could have done a better job of saying, was that innocence shouldn't be required of Black girls in order for us to receive respect and protection. If I could rewrite some of those words today—and this is my book, so I guess I can—what I would say is this:

We should be outraged and concerned about the bad things that happen to Black girls who are labeled as fast, whether the label is warranted or not. I agreed to have sex with an adult man when I was thirteen. To this day, I don't have any explanation for my eager participation, beyond the reality that at that age I got high on the excitement of sexual attention and energy. I also enjoyed the feeling of "getting away with" a secret sex life under the noses of the adults responsible for me. For all intents and purposes, I was fast. But the truth is that my reasonings don't matter. My neighbor is the one who should have to answer for his predatory behavior. He shouldn't have wanted to fuck me knowing that I was thirteen years old, no matter how much control I had over my schedule, what I wore, how I talked, how often he saw me sneaking hits off other boys' blunts, or if I sometimes had condoms in my cheap Rainbow purse. That shouldn't be a hard pill for grown ass men to swallow, but for some reason it is.

So Black girls have been forced to swallow it for them. We're expected to do the work for them, the work of shutting down our own sexualities so adults can't access them. Even now, as an adult who understands that I was preyed upon, I have to resist the urge to feel like I should have known better back then too. And therein lies the problem. I've internalized the idea that his predation was a direct result of me daring to have a sex life before I was old enough. I'm not asking for a seat at the table of victimhood, nor am I suggesting that anyone's chair be ripped from underneath them. I'm just hoping that someone is willing to go beyond how or why we became lil fast ass girls and instead consider what we need.

*　　*　　*

The informal sexual health advocacy and education work I did with my homegirls (and myself) in high school and college was actually an attempt to answer that question: What did sexually active Black girls and women need? I have never been interested in any interventionist approaches toward my sex life or that of any other Black girls. Despite any mistakes or fumbles on my part, I have never been ashamed of my sexuality. To the contrary, I've always found it freeing and exhilarating. It was often ground zero for the work I was doing to understand my different identities as a fat, Black, queer woman. I was a proud champion of the "Hoe is life" movement before the slogan ever made its way into social media. But before I got there, I had to answer that question for myself. I had to figure out what I needed.

With few other places to turn, I looked to the culture around me. There were the movies, like *Just Another Girl on the I.R.T.* and *Thirteen*. There were the books. I would gobble up Sister Souljah's *The Coldest Winter Ever*, Omar Tyree's *Flyy Girl*, and a bunch of other titles in the urban-fiction genre, trying to learn more about myself and what I wanted sexually. And then, of course, there was trap music and female rap. Those genres, and their sexually explicit content, were the most accessible to me. And they offered rich narratives and different perspectives on Black women's sexuality.

Rappers talk about women's bodies a lot, and not solely with the purpose of defining which among them is the most attractive. If you listen to enough rap, you'll hear them talk about stuff like abortions, the morning-after pill, condom usage, what pussies should smell like, and the anxiety over sexually transmitted diseases. Artists comment on how women should raise their kids, how their mothers raised them, the terms under which women should and shouldn't engage in sex. Hip-hop has always been a means of capturing the realities and fantasies of Black Americans, including our sex lives.

As such, I intuitively knew pretty early on that I couldn't trust men to dominate that conversation about women's bodies or issues. The heterosexual male gaze was often prioritized and drenched in ignorance. Even when I was in high school, I knew that healthy pussies should not ever smell like water. I knew that the morning-after pill was meant to be used as a backup method when other forms of contraceptives had failed, not as a way to have an abortion. I knew that no one should be able to dictate whether or not a woman carried her pregnancy to term.

Female rappers, on the other hand, opened up an entirely new world for me sexually. It's not that they operated completely outside that reductive male gaze. Most times they flourished in the spotlight of it. They performed feminine beauty in their music videos, interviews, and performances to advance their careers. They shape-shifted within and around the gaze, also using their sexuality as a source of power and leverage. They created a space for me to consider a framework wherein my desires and needs could come first. For a long time female rappers (and the characters in my favorite books and movies) were the only Black women—who were relatable and used accessible language that I could understand—encouraging me to define my own identity and sexuality. Female rappers helped me transition into a pleasure narrative. They were my entry point to feminism before I took gender studies courses in college and before I discovered the niche corners of Tumblr. Thanks to them, I set a new goal for myself in high school. After years of sneaking around with different boys (and men) for the hell of it, I wanted the shit to feel good, every time.

I started to reject the assumption that my partners were supposed to be the dominant party during sex, and I was more vocal about what felt good and what didn't. I wasn't afraid of being called a hoe for knowing what I liked, or for liking sex at all. I began to think of pleasure as something I could just go and get, not a lottery that I could hit if I was lucky.

With time and self-education through female rap, I really started to understand that Black women—even those of us who are fat, ghetto, trans, broke, young, and/or struggling— actually deserve pleasure. We deserve to feel good in our skin and in our relationships. We deserve to set our own boundaries and standards around sex. Unfortunately, too many of us learn the risks and damage our sexuality can cause, first. We learn about our own pleasure last, if we ever do. Yes, knowing that I've always had access to safe and legal contraceptives, abortion, and sexual health screenings has made me a better hoe. But I had to experience a lot of harm because I didn't have a strong framework of consent; supportive spaces where I could talk through some of my experiences with people other than my close group of peers; or a sex education curriculum that also incorporated compatibility, chemistry, and autonomy. Imagine the different decisions I could have made if I had. That's what I wanted, and still want for Black girls.

Because he'd helped so many Black women, I thought that following in Dr. J's footsteps would lead me to the solution. I assumed that if I was a gynecologist, I could combine scientific medical knowledge with my experiences as a Black woman in the trenches. I would be the hoe plug, just like my mama. However, I realized fairly quickly as an undergrad that I wasn't up for the challenge of eight years of scientific study that a medical degree requires. But even though the MD dreams were dead, my interest in the stories of Black women, their bodies, their sex lives, their relationships, and their communities was not. I wanted to advocate for Black girls not having to explore their sexuality in a culture of toxicity, tragedy, risk, harm, and fear. I understood that we needed resources, information, care, support, and respect, not judgment, retaliation, abuse, and disregard. By the time I got to college, I wasn't afraid to say that.

I took Dr. Ruth Nicole Brown's graduate class on Black girlhood when I was only a sophomore. She is the person who suggested that I apply to attend a leadership institute hosted by a pro-choice organization founded by Gloria Steinem, who was also there. Over the course of that weekend, I learned there was a name for the framework that made me such a loud advocate for Black women, and only Black women, determining what happened to them and their bodies: reproductive justice. Not only did I learn what reproductive justice is; I also left the event two days later equipped with the basics of how to organize around it. I dove in headfirst, kicking off six years of campus and professional work.

I was a sexual-assault awareness educator, facilitating required seminars for first-year students about sexual assault. I co-founded the only women-of-color-led, pro-choice organization on campus at the time. We threw lit ass events like birth-control parties and condom crawls, where we'd pass out condoms with messages about consent to students leaving the campus bars. We had legislative and campus wins around access to birth control. The following summer I headed to Washington, DC, to intern at the organization's headquarters, completely unaware that my student organization would win their Chapter of the Year award. I switched my major, for the second and final time, to gender and sexuality studies. When I moved back to Chicago, I did freelance work for the Chicago Abortion Fund. Everything had finally clicked into place and instilled in me a clear professional path forward and a renewed sense of passion.

Moving to Washington, DC, was, as I mentioned, the first step in my journey toward building real financial independence. But it was also the next step in continuing my advocacy work. I was at the very beginning of what I thought would be a career as a movement leader. But I abruptly ended my movement work in 2014, after being burnt out by the bureaucracy and pace. I knew that making it to the top of some huge nonprofit wasn't my calling either. Shortly after I moved to DC, I was selected to be a columnist for the now-defunct Feministing.com. Turns out I wouldn't be a movement leader, but I could be a movement voice, through my writing. Most of my writing career has been an exploration of Black girl sexuality, and I'm proud of that.

On top of my work duties, I wrote weekly pieces for the feminist blog covering women's issues and dissecting the imagery and roles of Black women in pop culture. I launched the sex column "Fucking with Feministing," where I educated readers on squirting, dildos, and polyamory. My tenure at Feministing .com coincided with another collision of feminism and pop culture, the first one since the third-wave "girl power" movement of the '90s. Olivia Pope was fucking the president and dominating prime-time television on *Scandal*. Miley Cyrus was twerking on Instagram and the MTV stage. Beyoncé, Rihanna, and Nicki Minaj represented a holy trinity of Black female dominance in the entertainment industry. Everyone, and everything, in pop culture seemed to be subjected to this question: Is this feminist? Meanwhile, as a graduate student at Georgia State University, I was writing a thesis on how Black girls and their sexuality were represented in memes on the internet. I also started to slowly but surely write love letters to female rappers framed as culture commentary. It was in the midst of all of this work that I birthed trap feminism and eventually started writing about it.

Trap feminism questions what sexual liberation can look like for Black girls when those bleak statistics are still a thing: Black women are disproportionately affected by intimate-partner violence and are most likely to be killed as a result of it. The lives of Black men are constantly deemed more important than ours. Black women have a higher maternal mortality rate. We are more likely to contract HIV. As children we are seen as less innocent and reprimanded more harshly in schools. Reproductive justice, which is about access, education, and a path toward liberation, was the vehicle for me to seek those answers and to combat the harmful narratives assigned to Dr. J's patients, to my homegirls, and to me. We've all been forced to navigate our sexuality in a world that says we shouldn't be doing it, and we've creatively rebelled anyway. We've figured the shit out on our own, and we continue to do so. We know what we need, even when it's hard to access.

Chapter 6

SELLING IT

Top notch hoes get the most, not the lesser.
> —UGK, "Int'l Players Anthem
> (I Choose You)," ft. Outkast[1]

He was a small and nerdy white man. Standing about two inches shorter than me, he was less than half my body weight for sure. When I opened the door to my studio apartment, he peered at me through thick-rimmed glasses with a giddy, boyish grin on his face. He looked exactly how I thought he would, based on the information he'd conveyed to me via email. I knew that he was married and that he worked in academia. The alignment of what he'd told me and his physical appearance put me at ease, especially after I assessed that I could easily beat his ass if he tried me. If he intended on putting me in danger, he would have to pull out a gun or find a way to drug me, otherwise he'd be leaving in need of medical attention. I smiled at him, greeting him warmly, like he was a high school crush I was seeing for the first time in years. All the while I was scanning his face, hands, and mannerisms for any signs of shiftiness. One flash of darkness in his eyes would have ruined everything and I would have started executing an abort mission.

A nosy neighbor could have easily passed him off as a co-worker or an IT guy, since it's unlikely that we hung out in similar circles. But I didn't even want to give anyone the chance to speculate so I hurried him in and shut the door behind him. After scanning him one more time, we finally touched when I offered him a top-heavy hug. I shivered a little as we separated. Partly because no matter how high I turned the heat up, I couldn't get rid of the winter chill in my cheap ass, poorly insulated apartment, but also because I was a little nervous. When I saw him put an envelope down on my table at an angle where I could see the contents inside, I relaxed a little. Once he was facedown and naked on the bed, with no gun and no roofies in sight, I relaxed a little bit more.

I stripped down to my underwear and started to massage his pasty skin with some of the surplus massage oil I had from my short-lived time as a sex-toy entrepreneur. After a few moments, he turned over. Through his little nerdy glasses, his eyes danced with excitement. He told me how good my hands felt. I smirked back at him and said, "Thank you." I worked my hands up his nimble thighs, and he let his head fall back onto the pillow. He was just as relieved as I was that this was going so smoothly. I didn't have anybody hiding in my closet with a gun, ready to rob him. I hadn't offered him a drink with drugs fizzing at the bottom of it. I was just a pretty, fat Black woman—with big titties spilling out of my bra, a soft double stomach within his arm's reach, and thighs that warmed his body up—giving him the massage he'd asked for.

With him on his back, I intentionally avoided touching his dick. Not because I was repulsed by the first white peen I'd ever seen this close or because I wasn't enjoying putting on this "performance" for him, but because I wanted to make the performance even better. I wanted to prolong his relaxation. I intuitively understood that, in this case, anticipation was an intoxicant. So I massaged my way up his thighs and then outward to his hips, letting my forearm barely graze the tip. Then I moved on to his torso and chest. I repeated this a few times, slowly, until his exhales transitioned into audible moans and his hips began to subtly shift. That's when I knew he was ready for his happy ending.

"You're incredible," he said when he was finished, propping himself up on one elbow and studying my face.

I thanked him, kissed his cheek, and began picking his clothes up off the floor and placing them on the bed next to him. It was time for him to go. The contents of that envelope were calling my name. I chatted him up as he got dressed. He was suddenly curious about me and my background: what I was studying, where I was from, and what I hoped to do after college. I made up fake answers to every question and told him to email me any time he wanted to come back. No more than twenty minutes had passed between him walking in and walking out of my frigid apartment. There was still enough time for me to make it to the bank and put the $150 he left me in that envelope into my account. My first job as a formal sex worker was done.

I don't talk a lot about my work as a professional dominatrix or escort for several reasons. The main one is that, despite it being the world's oldest profession, sex work is still illegal. The longer I've been out of the game, the more comfortable I am opening up about my history with it, without fear of anyone sending 12 to my door. But perhaps worse than the criminalization of sex work is the stigma around it. As a feminist writer who came up in the age of the personal narrative, I've talked about so much of my sex life on the internet for the world to see. I've talked about having casual sex, kinky sex, queer sex, and cyber sex, while racking up hundreds of thousands of views. None of those pieces has caused me the dread I feel when I think about my family reading *this* chapter, where I reference doing all of the freaky aforementioned for payment. Writing this feels very much like running headfirst and full speed toward a brick wall of preconceived notions about money, ethics, sexuality, self-worth, femininity, disgust, body image, morality, and shame that are all enmeshed in the idea of getting paid to fulfill someone else's fantasies.

My time as a sex worker allowed me to deeply interrogate many of the themes I've addressed in the book so far (body politics, lawlessness, confidence, money, sexuality) and others I'll write about later, but there might not be another chapter in this book that cuts more to the core of trap feminism than this one. Because there is no group that feels the impacts of racism, sexism, classism, transphobia, fat phobia, capitalism, criminalization, and state-sanctioned violence more directly than sex workers. This is even truer for those of us who are Black women, and especially for Black women who are trans. Trap feminism is very much a project that tries to make sense of this reality while bearing witness to a cultural obsession with sex work. For us to be so disgusted by and ashamed of women who get paid under the large umbrella of sex work, we damn sure can't look away.

All of this is why it was so important for me to finally engage with my own harlotry, publicly, even if I'm afraid I'm crossing the line that will actually get me disowned by my family. So here goes nothing.

*　　*　　*

On the rare occasions when I've discussed my *full* résumé to people, the first thing they want to know is: "How did you get into that?" They undoubtedly envision a seedy, secret underworld that feels distant and foreign, but sex work is actually a very common aspect of American culture. Julia Roberts became America's sweetheart for portraying a hoe with a heart of gold in *Pretty Woman*. Every few years an article goes viral about an Ivy League student who moonlights as an escort. (The most updated version of that story is that she makes thousands of dollars weekly as a cam girl.) The lines between the sugar-baby lifestyle and just "dating up" are steadily merging. On a collaboration track with Megan Thee Stallion, Beyoncé name-dropped OnlyFans, a subscription-based site where creators can share exclusive, and sometimes sexually explicit, content with their fan base. In Black pop culture, the student by day is a stripper by night, a trope that is still going just as strong today as it was when LisaRaye played Diamond in *The Players Club* in 1998. Today's female rap thrives on the premise that niggas who can't afford to do so don't get to fuck bad bitches. The nickname for this genre is "stripper rap."

Even outside media, transactional sex is way more common than any of us are willing to admit. Our practices around sex, dating, relationships, and marriage often extend beyond our primal desire to simply connect with a person we love. We usually want, negotiate, and receive *something* that is of value to us in return for performing sexuality. The girl who looks forward to the free meals that come from her Tinder dates because she just moved to New York City and money is still a little tight is leveraging the sexual desire of her potential partners to get her needs met. Your homegirl who won't sleep with the person she's dating (even though she really wants to) because she's trying to lock down a relationship or romantic commitment is essentially bartering sex for a sense of security and trust. The broke ass nigga who comes over to fuck but ends up staying at your house for weeks at a time while he's in between places is slanging dick for housing, sis. Even when we fuck someone just to get a nut off, we're just trading our nut for theirs (hopefully). It's a transaction. This is why I intentionally use words like "professional" and "formal" when talking about being a sex worker, to delineate when I was actually marketing and offering my services in this arena and when I was just a regular degular hoe, getting people (myself included) off because it was fun.

The transition from broke hoe to pro hoe was another way that I established my own worth against a backdrop of messaging that I was worthless in sexual contexts. When people ask how I got into sex work, it's often coming from the same space of confusion that leads people to ask me how I became so confident. They're not interested in the specific steps I took to set up a side business as a provider of erotic experiences, unless they want to be a hoe too. They're curious about how a fat Black girl who is supposed to be happy and grateful when anyone is attracted to her ended up in a position where people would *pay* to engage with her sexually. They want to know how the laws of fat phobia were skirted in order for me to tap into a market of people who not only found me attractive but also found my time and my body to be worth a monetary amount. In the spirit of transparency, when I first got into sex work, I wanted answers to these questions as well.

I was in the thick of that confidence journey when I started professional hoeing. I was just starting to realize that being fat wasn't the burden I had thought it was, that my body was just one variation of body among billions, and that I could inhabit my own version of sexiness. I knew people were attracted to me—that had always been the case—but I was owning that I was *attractive*. This coincided with a deepened understanding of gender, sexuality, reproductive justice, and body autonomy that I was receiving thanks to my coursework and campus

want smoke:

Similar to "with the shits," which implies that you're down for whatever, wanting smoke means that you're not afraid of confrontation or the consequences of any resulting altercation.

organizing. I viewed sexual repression as a form of control over women's bodies, and I was actively trying to rid myself of a lot of the stigma associated with sex. I wanted all the smoke with taboos, especially the ones that were placed on my body as a fat Black girl. Plus, I was broke, and one of the only other things occupying my energy at the time was keeping up with my bills.

There's a saying that the "hoe shit" ain't on you, it's in you. Some people are just cut out for the lifestyle because they have the right cocktail of skills, emotional capacity, sexual openness, experience, and circumstance. I fully believe that, because the hoe shit was definitely in me. I didn't have any of the moral hang-ups that lead people to turn their noses up at hoes. I was street-smart, could sense danger, and knew how to keep my cool under pressure. I knew how to finesse. Most important, the timing was right. I needed the money and was more than willing to perform all kinds of different versions of femininity when I knew there was cash waiting for me at the end of the tunnel. All of this was true of me before I ever *consciously* engaged in any kind of transactional sex, and together they were the catalyst that got me into the game.

My homegirls and I were having one of our deep conversations late one night. We were kiki'ing around the table when the topic of our early twenties financial woes came up. One of my friends was trying to make a joke when she said: "I'm so broke I'd do something strange for a piece of change right now." (In the early aughts, doing something "strange for a piece of change" was how you talked about hoeing if you weren't trying to actually be mean-spirited or whore phobic.) It was meant to be cheeky, but she didn't laugh when she said it, and she cast her eyes away from us as the words left her mouth. It was clear that deep down she meant every word. She just wasn't sure how we'd react. But she would get no judgment here. Instead, she was met with a chorus of "Shiiiid, me too!" from myself and our other friends. None of us were laughing either.

We didn't know *how* to do it, but we knew we were down to do it, and we were emboldened by the circle of trust we'd built. Our first idea was to see if one of us could win an amateur-night prize at a local strip club we'd visited before, and we'd all split the prize money. A few weeks later, the four of us piled into Sandy with our bags packed, ready to cross state lines for a quick come up. When we arrived at the club, my friends who were going to compete waited before they signed up. It was a smart move because after watching the first few contestants go up, we realized they weren't amateurs at all. These dancers were professionals from other strip clubs who had the same idea to make a stack. My friends' chances of winning were slim.

None of us wanted to let the night go to waste, though. We chilled in the spot, enjoying free drinks and bomb ass fried chicken. (Fun fact: a strip club is only as good as the fried chicken it serves.) Some guys who had been eyeing our crew since we walked in were taking care of the tab. We huddled together and decided that we could take our chances on a more personalized lick. There were four of us, we had one another's backs, and these dudes looked pretty harmless. So we offered them the opportunity for a private show back at their place, and got them out of the club before they blew any more money on strippers. At their two-bedroom apartment in a forgettable complex, my homegirls proved that they were not amateurs at everything. I made sure everyone was okay and held on to the money until it was time to go. It wasn't nearly as much as we'd hoped to make on our little come-up trip, and Sandy smelled like badussy for the whole trip home, but we still get a damn good laugh out of it. None of us were the hustlers or hoes we would eventually become, but we certainly made some good memories.

I would hardly consider this my formal introduction to sex work, but it was definitely what got the ball rolling. As it turns out, my friends were with the hoe shit, but they didn't need the money as much as I did, and they weren't as curious about exploring their own sexual politics like I was. So I kept going while they stayed at the ready. I dove headfirst into research and found that my new side hustle was just a few pics and a couple of clicks on the internet away. I posted my first ad, and that's how the nerdy white guy ended up at my crib getting a massage with a happy ending.

If we're being technical, the answer to the question "How did you get into sex work?" is: the internet. Anyone with a phone can snap some pictures of themselves, decide on an hourly rate, and put it all on a relevant website or forum with their contact information. It was decidedly easier before the extremely harmful SESTA (Stop Enabling Sex Traffickers Act) was passed in 2018, but back when I started it was as simple as that. There

badussy:

Describes the specific aroma that results
from the meeting of butt, dick, and pussy.

were plenty of resources available to anyone who had the time to do some internet sleuthing on which sites would be best to market and advertise your services, figure out pricing, and what language to use in ads.

To actually learn the ropes and navigate this world, though, I had to get to know other women in the industry. My first attempts at joining the community of professional dominatrixes—which I thought would be a safer bet, legally—were unsuccessful. As ridiculous as it sounds, there is a bit of whore phobia even within sex work. Sometimes providers who offer only visual and audio sensory services (like phone sex operators, cam girls, and strippers who abide by no-contact rules) think they're better than those who offer more. And some of the providers who offer contact services (like kink providers and erotic-massage givers) think they have a moral high ground over sex workers who provide full service, or sex, to their clients. And even among full-service providers there is elitism from those who work online, at higher rates, and with privileged backgrounds toward those who work the streets, who have pimps, those struggling with addiction, or those who work at lower rates and under riskier circumstances to ensure their own survival. In many ways this internal whore phobia has merged with the purism of some BDSM practitioners, and the result is a strong wariness toward folks who are interested in making money in the lifestyle. Many pro-dommes build their professional reputations on the fact that they've been part of the lifestyle in a nonprofessional capacity first, and they tend to be suspicious of newbies, especially young Black women, stepping onto the scene. So despite the fact that I had a genuine interest—and talent, if I do say so myself—for dominating men, I never did get a good foothold in the kink community, officially.

This snobbish exclusivity did not exist among escorts. Many of them were women who, just like me, simply had the hoe shit in them. Not long after I started posting ads and interacting on some of the boards, I was in regular communication with several women I shared clients with or I had chatted with in forums. These women were moms, they were students, they were orphans, they had disabilities, they were young profes-sionals. Some of them were out to their families and friends and organized on behalf of sex worker rights; a lot of them kept this part of their lives a complete secret from everyone. A few of them—the ones who were some combination of white, thin, and able-bodied—made thousands of dollars per week traveling to luxurious destinations all around the world with designer bags on their arms. Others barely made enough to support themselves and their families but had extenuating cir-cumstances that made it difficult to secure other kinds of work. Most of us were somewhere in the middle. In good weeks, we might make our rent in a single day, but that might be followed by weeks without booking a single client. The common thread among us was that we were doing the best we could with what we had and trying to stay out of harm's way while we did it.

We relied on one another for that. We used one another for client references, confirming that the men who reached out to us were who they said they were. We acted as one another's safety contact—the person who receives information on where you are, whom you're with, and how long you should be there—when we couldn't tell our friends and families what we did for a living. We shared which hotels were provider friendly and which ones kept track of traffic in and out of a room. We used whisper networks to warn other girls about law-enforcement stings, scammers, and predators to avoid. We had hoe brunches just to vent and fellowship with one another. Some of these women are still friends of mine. Some of them are still sex workers, keeping me abreast of how women are navigating an already delicate industry with a pandemic and the stricter rules in online advertising. These women gave me my education in sex work best practices. It's because of their wisdom that I never again hosted a client at my own place, like I did with that first nerdy client. They taught me how to build my brand and market myself (which was super important as a plus-size provider), and how to retain clients and build a base of regulars (the secret sauce is to take the time to get to know your clients and invest in making them think that you would fuck them for free). We swapped tricks on how to maximize our time with clients (prolong foreplay and control their orgasm so they'll want to stay longer, or spend more money) and get rid of the ones who were annoying (set your phone alarm so that it sounds like your ringtone and fake an emergency). Makeup tips. Period sex. Bitcoin. Hoes taught me all of that. But most important, they taught me how to really step into my confidence and stand on a foundation of self-preservation and personal progress.

Sex work is where I saw, in real time, so much of the Black, queer, feminist, body, gender, and sexuality theory I had studied enacted in real life. I really started to understand desirability politics as a product of access and socialization. For example, most of my clients were professional white men in their forties and fifties. Their opportunities to engage with fat Black women at their Ivy League schools, their corporate jobs, or their mostly white neighborhoods were slim or none. I was able to deduce from their interactions with me that the reason there is a widely held belief that "people aren't attracted to fat Black women" is because fat Black women do not fit into the imagined normative lifestyle of these privileged men. We simply do not exist in their world. People engage with their desires only as much as their lives and communities allow them to. Even within our intimate relationships, many of us are performing gender, sexuality, and desire in the ways that are expected of us, not in ways that reflect the full spectrum of our sexual interests.

Contrary to what people think about men who patronize sex workers, they're not desperate creeps who can't get sex anywhere else. They're men who want to have sex that they have to go somewhere else, literally and figuratively, to get. They're looking for specific experiences that meet their specific needs, experiences that allow them to explore those fringe corners of their desires. Providers offer them the space and chance to tap into those parts of their sexuality that they're not able to express in their everyday lives. We fill holes that would have gone untended to otherwise, holes that aren't always explicitly sexual. While sex work is often reduced to sucking and fucking, sex workers also do a ton of emotional and mental labor for clients. Desire, romance, and intimacy are holistic experiences and not skin-deep. I've had clients who never even saw me fully nude because they were interested in an erotic experience that wasn't limited to penetration. Many of my clients simply wanted to relish a lack of control. (Side note: I really miss being mean to white men for money. They need it now more than ever. Any cash pigs reading this, holla at me, you piece of shit.) Some of them were just too busy to commit to dating.

It was my job to get to know my clients, to understand what they needed, even when they didn't. I had to ensure that I was embodying a body-positive lens to make room for clients with different body types and abilities. I had to be detail oriented and listen. I had to trust my gut. I learned, for the first time, how fulfilling it could be to act in the service of someone else. The better I got at this, the more fulfilling the work was for me. It probably sounds weird, but being a hoe pushed me to be a better person and a better partner in general. Every envelope full of cash was an affirmation of what I had to offer the world.

Most important, though, I understood that having romantic access to me is a privilege, a luxury, even. Freed from the respectability politics that supported this line of thinking, I was able to rethink my own value in my dating life, which I'll talk more about in a later chapter. Yes, sex work is a threat to capitalism because of the financial autonomy it offers in a system that relies on disenfranchised folks as a labor force. But it also poses a threat to the established power dynamic that tends to work against Black femmes in romantic contexts. We are indoctrinated to think that our time, bodies, and energy are worth only as much as our partners say they are. We're taught that the only outcomes we should expect for sharing these parts of ourselves is the companionship of someone else. Hoes know better than that. We know that it takes real work to satisfy someone else's needs, work that has material value.

When critics try to insult female rappers by comparing them to sex workers (like when during a *Love & Hip Hop* reunion episode Peter Gunz said that if a woman wants to be treated to cash or gifts before agreeing to have sex, she's prostituting herself), they're underestimating the inherent power that sex workers possess: the power of self-determination. That's why new spitters like Sukihana lean into their hoeism. That's why, despite these critiques, so many female rappers still insist that anyone who wants to fuck them is going to have to pay the tax. There are few things that make me feel as empowered as I do when I'm listening to a Black woman talk about how expensive her pussy is. They might not have websites created to lure a certain clientele, but their Instagram accounts work just as well, and I'm sure the DMs are booming.

* * *

It's important that I talk about my stint as a sex worker—a positive, autonomous experience that helped me stay afloat financially for a number of years before I had a viable career—because that's not the narrative we typically get about sex workers, especially Black women. The media wants you to believe that sex work is seedy. Themes of desperation, force, trafficking, and violence are recycled there, depicting a shadowy underground that snatches souls and never returns them. A lot of rappers want us to believe that sex work is sexy. Neither is the definitive truth, but it can be both. It doesn't matter if we're not hearing about the experiences of sex workers, good or bad, from those in the field. Sex work shouldn't be co-opted for shocking headlines or catchy bars.

I've heard horror stories of providers being robbed and raped. Trans women who are pushed into survival sex work are at an even higher risk of violence. It cannot be understated how epidemics like gender-based violence, homophobia, transphobia, and addiction (just to name a few) collide with income inequality and lead women to pursue sex work. I also understand there is a completely different sector of the industry in which women and girls are coerced into prostitution by other people. I'm particularly sensitive to this reality because a decade before I was making money as a sex worker I was almost one of those girls.

When I was fourteen, a close friend of the family—let's call him D—asked me if I was a virgin. We'd just pulled into a parking lot near the projects that operated as his stomping grounds. As we drove past crackheads and corner boys, D slowed the car down and turned 8Ball & MJG's "Mr. Big" up to its maximum volume. He was clearly feeling himself as he drove (a car that wasn't his) through the narrow streets leading into one of the Chicago housing complexes that have since been torn down. But before he'd inquired about my sexual activity, he turned the car off and the radio all the way down. I knew this was not passing curiosity of an adult trying to offer support or guidance. It was a pitch. Before I could even answer, he continued with a spiel about how I could and should be "getting money from these niggas" if I was going to deal with them at all.

D and I were spending more time together than usual, which is what led to this sly proposition in the car. He would sometimes try to impress me with gifts or stories about how much money he had. On other occasions, I would ride along with him on random trips (he didn't have a job so they were indeed random). We were usually running errands, but sometimes we would stop to hang out at the homes of his friends. During one of these outings, he asked me in front of all of his old ass cronies if I had brushed my teeth that day. It was a weird question, but before I could respond, he grabbed my face, pulled it close to his, and ran his tongue across my front teeth. I was disgusted and made that very clear as I pulled away. He just laughed and sent me back into another room, giving a knowing look to his friends.

Even at that age, the idea of prostitution wasn't foreign to me. I knew there were some women who were willing to have sex with men for money. I also knew there were pimps, men who made money off those women. These dynamics showed up in the music I listened to and some of the series and movies I watched. Pimp culture is also extremely prominent in the Midwest, especially in places like Chicago and Detroit. But whenever I witnessed this culture, it was explicitly named. Terms like "prostitution," "hooker," and "turning tricks" seemed to draw a line in the sand that defined what hoeing was and was not. They were labels that identified a group of women who had been written off as shameful and amoral. D was giving me creep vibes, for sure, but he hadn't used any of those terms or described those dynamics. I'd brushed him off after his speech in the car because by the time I was fourteen I already felt a sense of ownership over my own sexuality. Involving D or any other adult in it just wasn't appealing to me. But it definitely wasn't because I'd realized exactly what he was up to.

D was trying to turn me out, slowly but surely. With all of the gifts, the stories about how much money he supposedly had, the unsolicited questions and "advice" he had about my sex life, and the time he suddenly wanted us to spend together, D was grooming me. He already thought of himself as a pimp; he just needed a woman at his behest to complete that fantasy. When he stuck his tongue into my mouth in front of those other men, invading my personal space and my body, he was trying to give them the impression that he had power over my body, even though he didn't. If he'd had his way, some of those same men would have paid him for a chance to do more than "check" my teeth. The only reason it stopped was because not long after these incidents, I went to live with my grandparents and D went to prison. I don't know how far things would have gone if there hadn't been physical distance put between us. I know hindsight is 20/20, but if I knew then what I know now, I would have bitten his fucking tongue off.

When I hear news stories about underage girls being trafficked, I know exactly how easy it is. Had D been an older dude from the neighborhood whom I had a crush on, a neighbor I was creeping around with, or someone I felt closer to, I could have easily been turned out. If I'd had a boyfriend who told me this was what he wanted me to do for him, I can see how my fourteen-year-old brain could have found ways to justify it. Had I been one of those fourteen-year-old girls who are treated like surrogate heads of their households and feel an obligation to make some money for their families, and not just for a new purse, D's proposition could have sounded like music to my ears. While it may seem easy to identify pimps when they're dressed like Bishop Don Juan, and hoes when their asses are jutting out from the sides of cars on the street, it looks different for young girls who get caught up in the game. It looks like an abusive boyfriend, expectations from older family members, or being a down ass bitch riding for the rich older guy you're "dating."

These stories of exploitation, violence, and despondency are often used as justification for the criminalization of sex work. In case you're one of those people, I'm here to tell you why you're way off base. First and foremost, let's get on the same page that consensual sex work is not the same thing as sex trafficking. It's like the difference between consensual sex and rape. Sex work involves consenting parties negotiating the terms under which they engage in sex. Trafficked individuals cannot give consent because they're acting under the authoritarian rule of someone else. Trying to combat sex trafficking by criminalizing the entire sex trade is like trying to regulate sex in order to prevent rape.

Industries like agriculture and domestic work are also hotspots for trafficking, but there haven't been any attempts to ban hiring migrant workers or live-in housekeepers. Those sectors are allowed to exist, and there are rules, laws, and task forces in place to help curb those who would take advantage of workers. The most present danger that sex workers navigate is law enforcement. We have to figure out ways to advertise, screen clients, and serve clients without drawing the attention of the police or walking into a sting. If crimes are committed against us while we're working, we put our own freedom at risk in the pursuit of justice. Dirty cops are among the predators we may encounter. On top of all that, the economic consequences of entering the criminal justice system makes it more likely that we will have to continue to pursue sex work, which was the case for me after my arrest.

Decriminalizing sex work would make it safer for sex workers to do their jobs, and easier to fight trafficking. This hasn't happened because not only are we still tied to conservative attitudes about the circumstances under which people have sex but also because people refuse to acknowledge that sex work is real work. The bottom line for all sex workers is the dollar. Sex work can be dangerous, but so can construction.

People can exploit it like they can anything else. For many sex workers they would be doing something else if they had the choice, and I think a bunch of Walmart employees would say the same thing. People are drawn to this underground economy in a system that doesn't provide nearly enough help or resources to those who need it most. Rather than address the issues that make sex work a viable option for so many, like a livable wage and reliable protection against gender-based violence and homophobia, we've continued to put an already vulnerable workforce even more at risk.

And still, sex work is alive and well. It still offers women the opportunity for financial freedom and personal growth. The internet gave sex workers more than access to a global community and a means to express themselves and raise awareness; it also gave them even more ways to make money. Sex work is still forcing us to reconsider our assumptions about different bodies and forms of sexual expression. It's also still hiding in plain sight via the sex we have every day outside the official bounds of the industry. I am not suggesting that this is the only means of accomplishing any of the above, but it's a model that should be taken more seriously, for sure. I'm not saying that everyone should go out and get their hoe credentials, but I don't think it's a terrible idea to consider how much hoe shit is already in you.

Chapter 7

NOT STRAIGHT

Came with my niggas and left with a baddie.

—DreamDoll, "Ah Ah Ah"[1]

My mama took me to my first Pride celebration when I was around fifteen, but she refused to tell me what it was. "We're going to a picnic!" she said, exasperated, whenever I asked her about the day's plans. I knew she was on some kind of bullshit, but I couldn't put my finger on what was going on. We weren't the kind of mama-daughter duo that would just go on random picnics to spend quality time together. But she was putting on makeup and had an outfit picked out for the occasion. I was expected to get cute too. When I pressed her about who was hosting this event or what the theme of it might be—it could have been a birthday party, a family reunion, or an outdoor work potluck for all I knew—she doubled down on the fact that it was just . . . a picnic. This was still a few years before social media and the internet were a major part of our lives, so I had no clue that it was Pride weekend in Chicago. I just had to ride along wherever my mama took me and take in the day's events as they unfolded.

The "picnic" was at a beach park on the South Side, and I realized almost immediately why my mama was being so weird about the shit. First of all, "picnic" was clearly an understatement. There were hundreds of people in attendance, and rainbow-colored paraphernalia was everywhere. Smoke from portable barbecue grills, blunts, and Newport cigarettes rose above the sea of moving Black bodies. Several speaker systems and boom boxes competed for dominance over a crowd that was eating, drinking, talking, laughing, dancing, and maneuvering from one part of the grassy area to another. Despite the colorful rainbows, I noticed pretty quickly that there weren't a lot of other kids there. There were hardly any men there either. (At least there weren't a lot of people I would have labeled as men. Knowing what I know now about gender, I recognize that my teen interpretation of anyone's gender wasn't necessarily aligned with their actual gender identity.) I tried not to stare at the few people I read as men who strutted by me in jeans with pockets cut completely out, exposing their butt cheeks, or with full faces of makeup, and glitter cascading down their exposed chests, past chains that connected their nipple rings. The majority of the partygoers were women, and many of them were masculine-presenting studs.

One of those studs was my mama's girlfriend, whom I'd already met. As much as I would love to brag that my mama was being proactive about immersing me in queer culture or exposing me to different sides of life, I don't think it was that deep. She actually had no clue how I would react to that environment, but she wanted to kick it with her boo and their friends. This wasn't an event for me, which is why she didn't want to tell me where we were going. My mama never sat me down and had a conversation with me about her sexuality. There just came a time after she and my dad broke up when she dated women, specifically studs. I almost respect her more for taking this approach. There would have been nothing I could do or say to change how she felt about the people she loved and fucked; it was just something I had to accept. (More homophobes need that energy, but I digress.) I guess my mama assumed that if I didn't speak out in protest of her lifestyle, there was nothing to talk about. And she was right. I would just have to deal. But I never did have a problem with the fact that my mom liked women. Any issues I've ever had with the people my mama dated had nothing to do with their gender identity or sexual orientation.

She would get no such protests from me at that first Pride either. Even though it was for grown folks, I was excited by the outlandish outfits and pure joy surrounding me. Being around so many queer people wasn't disgusting or offensive to me. But I *was* scared that I would be perceived as one of them. At that age, I thought I was straight. And in case you haven't heard, heterosexuality is insecure and extremely fragile. It needs to be performed and defended at all costs. It's basically the short cis man of the sexuality spectrum. Add that to my inflated teenage ego, and my primary source of discomfort was that someone would think that I, too, was "family." I didn't have a problem with queer people, but I was not ready to be called one. I wondered how shooting the shit at Pride might somehow stain my record. This fear kicked into overdrive when two of my male classmates recognized me in the crowd. I loudly exaggerated the fact that my mama had *dragged* me to the event with her friends, and they truly didn't give two fucks about it. They offered a few more niceties and went right on their way. In fact, I was so busy deflecting that I hardly noticed what a hurry they seemed to be in to get away from me. And I didn't even think to ask them what *they* were doing there.

Attending Pride for the first time helped me begin to understand there was such a thing as a queer community. It normalized being queer in a major way for me. I had definitely seen gay people before this moment: There was obviously my mama and her partners. There was a flamboyantly gay man I occasionally ran into at the corner store. There was a fine ass stud I'd noticed playing basketball with guys at a park. I've had gay classmates, consistently, since the seventh grade. But I thought of all these people as isolated entities. Gay people were talked about in only one of two ways back in those days. They were either mentioned in hushed tones and whispers by straight people or scandalously caricatured on media like *The Jerry Springer Show* and *The Jenny Jones Show*. They certainly weren't treated with dignity or respect, or welcomed as members of the community. So it was easy to dismiss them and their lifestyle as one-off exceptions to the laws of physical attraction.

However, the sheer number of Black queer women at Pride

proved it was highly unlikely to be as uncommon or under-ground as I had thought. The picnic was just a few minutes' drive from the hood. These Black folks hadn't been bussed in from other parts of town. They were from these very same neighborhoods. Perhaps they weren't dressed in the same out-fits they would wear to school or work, but they were flexing no less. I made it a point after my first-ever Pride to pay even closer attention to the Black folks I witnessed expanding the norms of gender and sexuality beyond binaries. I wondered who I may have overlooked, how many queer folks I was living amongst I just couldn't read or "clock"? I left Pride knowing without a doubt that there were already gays in the trap. There still are.

*   *   *

The advent of raunchy female rap in the late '90s saw women playing with themes of lesbianism and bisexuality in their rec-ords. Artists like Queen Latifah, Da Brat, and Missy Elliott used their personal style and aesthetics to sidestep the con-straints of the gender binary without ever touching on their own queerness. That has given way to rappers, like DreamDoll, who are even more explicit about their sexcapades with women and sleeping with people's wives. When Young M.A dominated the charts for months after she dropped "OOOUUU," straight men scratched their heads, trying to figure out how she could be getting deep throated.

While I would never seek to minimize the impact of queer Black women in hip-hop, I think the crown jewel of radical representation in the game these days has been femme gay rappers. Take Saucy Santana, the ultra-femme rapper from Tallahassee, as an example. A makeup artist, internet sensation, and close friend of City Girls' Yung Miami, Santana helped set my entire summer 2020 mood with the release of his album *Pretty Little Gangsta.* In skintight dresses and with fully contoured cheekbones on top of a moisturized beard, he shakes ass while rapping about walking men like dogs and being a "material girl." Coming up behind him is teenage sensation Kidd Kenn from Chicago. He easily gives Barbie's Ken doll a run for his money with perfectly contoured eyebrows and a well-kept fade that is often dyed different colors of the rainbow. Kenn raps with a cadence and drawl similar to Queen Key, bragging about taking people's boyfriends and being who he is without consequence. Both of them have cult followings because they play on themes similar to those that have made female rap so seductive for generations of Black women: empowerment, confidence, pride, and powerful femininity. They're securing bags and deals in the process. We have come a long way from the Freaky Boiz going viral on YouTube back in 2010 for putting their spin on Gucci Mane's "Freaky Girl."

The veil has also been lifted on the presence of queer folks behind the scenes in hip-hop. Tokyo Stylez, Arrogant Tae, Alonzo Arnold, and Jonathan Wright are part of an elite squad of wig slayers. None of them are on the cis, heterosexual end of the gender spectrum. Their clientele—and friend lists—includes female rappers, strippers, and other industry women. A similar task force dominates fashion, with figures like Law Roach, Shane Justin, E. J. King, and Todd White. This says nothing of the queer photographers, writers, and editors who also help shape how trap culture is defined.

Trap culture's claim on heterosexuality has never been as strong as its cis men have tried to make it seem. The gender bending and queer signaling in trap culture is stronger than ever, even among its cis, straight men. The queer vibes were strong during Young Thug's creatively androgynous phase. It included a full editorial photo shoot with a dress and a tutu, and his practice of happily referring to his homeboys as "lover" and "bae." Atlanta rapper Gunna didn't think twice about proudly rocking a big ass Chanel purse to carry thousands of dollars in cash, and a cell phone. That shoulder shimmy Lil Uzi Vert is known for always gives me "Hey, girl!" energy. Federal informant Tekashi69 is a client of Jonathan Wright now. Upon his release from prison, he had a full lace wig installed in rainbow colors. For comedy's sake, Lil Yachty has no problem dressing like Oprah, painting his nails, and flat-ironing his hair. Even as these men uphold heterosexuality, they're pushing against the rigidity of masculinity in ways they don't even realize.

Even the parts of trap culture that are supposed to fall within the boundaries of heterosexuality are actual performances of a version of sexuality that falls outside Westernized heterosexuality. Professor LaMonda Horton-Stallings is the one who put me onto this in her quintessential article "Hip-Hop and the Black Ratchet Imagination." She looked, specifically, at the place of strip clubs in the creative lexicon of hip-hop, which was an excellent focal point. We have strip-club anthems, strip clubs as the sites to test new trap music, strippers as prototypes for Black women's bodies, and strip clubs as spaces of sexual desire. (I would add that I don't think it's a surprising development that strip-club patronage is now an expression of wealth and success for both men *and* women in the industry.) Horton-Stallings pointed out that the dynamics between patrons and dancers are actually way off script for Westernized sexual narratives, and we know it. We may not name it as such because we've reduced queerness itself to a set of specific sex acts, but throwing money with your homeboys in a crowded room to see women dance in a way that is unique to Black people is definitely queer. The same is true of shaking ass for money in the first place, which inspires that kind of voyeurism.

But trap culture thrives by giving a middle finger to these conservative ideals that require sexual purity for upstanding citizen status. Name me a trap song about a private, one-on-one sexual encounter between a married man and woman. I'll wait. With every track, artists find ways to revel in the pleasures of casual sex, transactional sex, communal sex, and kinky sex. Horton-Stallings argued that the creative expression of these kinds of desires is actually a performance of failure:[2] failure to fully assimilate, failure to accept rules about how we should be fucking . . . rules that also uphold heterosexuality. Even if trap culture doesn't actively promote this failure to adhere, it is constantly performing it in different ways.

When Black people see gay characters on television and assume there's some kind of "gay agenda" being used to influence the masses, I call bullshit. When they argue that treating queer people with humanity, friendliness, and courtesy is a struggle because there were never "this many" queer folks before, I call bullshit. When grown ass men and women shrink at the very mention of queer people or queer issues, I call bullshit. I side-eye every last one of those #BlackLove Instagram pages that preach unity and community but don't feature any queer or nonbinary couples. Trans women are being murdered by cishet men who know them and know that they are trans. Black queer kids are being kicked out of their homes by their Black parents and Black relatives. We see Black queer and trans folks; we know Black queer and trans folks. We make a choice about how we treat them, and the unfortunate reality is that as more of them express themselves online, see themselves represented in media, and find community with one another, they are sometimes just being met with more violence. We want them to think they don't belong, but queerness is not foreign to Black culture.

The real tea is that our backward allegiance to heterosexuality is actually a function of white supremacy. That rigid masculinity Black cis men are supposed to embody is one-half of a gender binary set up to uphold the moral superiority of our colonizers. It supports an equally rigid nuclear family

tea:

The LGBTQ community popularized the
phrase "spill the tea," which means to share
the gossip, news, and/or information.

model that leaves little room for communal living and support of one another. Families that break off into insular units are modeled after our society of individuals who fall into different groups or classes of people but aren't required to support other people within those groups. People are worried about the gay agenda when an imperialist agenda pushed us into straight-gay/man-woman binaries that were never meant for us and our communities in the first place. Our own internalized anti-Blackness has led us to believe that Black excellence comes only in the form of heterosexual marriage, kids, and wealth building. Because our survival as Black folks in Westernized culture often depends on our ability and willingness to succeed under these moral codes, we've embraced those heteronormative, binary rules and incorrectly processed them as part of some natural order. But sexuality exists on a spectrum, and there is nothing natural about the compulsive heterosexuality we impose on ourselves and others, which is exactly why hip-hop, especially trap culture, has low-key rebelled against it.

"Hip-Hop and the Black Ratchet Imagination" was an absolute game changer for me when I was piecing together how queerness was also part of trap feminism. I knew that its scope went beyond hip-hop's historical homophobia and exclusion of queer people. It also wasn't enough to simply document emerging queer artists as examples of burgeoning representation and progress. This framing of "failure" and queerness offered me room to look deeper at sex work, marginalized bodies, and lawlessness. I was already interested in trap culture as a critique and resistance against Western morality and hierarchies, so Horton-Stallings's queer reading helped me deconstruct and de-center heterosexuality as foundational to it.

*　　*　　*

As a cisgender femme, I've experimented with several different labels around my sexual orientation. First, I simply identified as "not straight." But that's like identifying as "not white." It doesn't illustrate what you actually are and places whiteness as the baseline to which everything else is compared. It was important to me to de-center heterosexuality when figuring out how to define myself. "Bisexual" truly wasn't broad enough for me, even though I do identify with a lot of the struggles they face around erasure and mistrust both inside and outside the queer community. "Pansexual" ultimately felt too pretentious and seemed to invite deep theoretical conversations, even when I wasn't trying to have them. Any time I found myself having to explain it to someone, I felt like one of those people who put "sapiosexual" in their Tinder bio. At the time of this writing, "queer" works the best for me. But "not straight" will always have a place in my heart because that defined what set me on my journey.

Sure, I'd been playing house across the gender spectrum since I was little, but I had no social or cultural scripts, no points of reference, for how to process my attraction to girls, let alone date them. As I mentioned, there wasn't much acknowledgment of queer relationships, let alone narratives that normalized queer attraction. I feel like I've been indoctrinated to like boys since I was extremely young, something that is true for a lot of Black women. From the fairy tales we read and watched to the obsession with whose mom was still with their dads, the bottom line was that being romantically tethered to a boy defined what it meant to be a girl. By the time I was ten years old, the pursuit of male attention was so ingrained in the psyches of my friends and I that it felt like a sport. We'd chat endlessly about which boy was the cutest, who liked whom, if the feelings were reciprocated, and how to act on those feelings. This was our version of an NCAA bracket. The game just got more intense as we grew older, had more freedom, had stronger personalities, and sex was thrown into the mix. But at every stage of development, we all were expected to play and keep up with the rules as best we could. We didn't have coaches or captains, just an unofficial rule book that outlined how we were supposed to look, feel, act, and be in order to "win."

Online there is a growing subculture of Black women who are invested in reconnecting with their "feminine energy" and "leveling up." They meet at the place where dating coaching and Black entrepreneurship intersect online. Leveling up is synonymous with being more attractive to would-be suitors, and part of leveling up involves nailing a certain aesthetic. It's not uncommon for dating coaches to not only offer tips for how to meet "better quality" men but also offer advice on how to look the part. From the way they wear their hair to their home decor, the way they speak, and their interest in topics like financial literacy, the process is supposed to help them become women of substance.

At the surface, this isn't the worst thing in the world. I, too, think you're a badder bitch when you look good and have your coin together. I love to see Black women leveled up. But I definitely peep how this process is often about moving further away from any traits associated with being too ghetto or hood, and equated with some idealized version of "femininity." I have noticed how some of these hurdles outlined in this version of that same rule book are harder to overcome for some Black women because of their education, class background, physical abilities, or body type.

As a fat Black girl, the game was never meant to work in my favor. Still, I desperately wanted to play and benefit from the privileges that came from winning at it. I took advantage of every opportunity to be in the presence of boys, and I let my walk and my voice change when I was. The decision between wearing my hair in a wrap or slicking it down into a side ponytail with some black gel often came down to what I thought looked more "feminine." But most notably, I ignored my attraction to people who weren't men. Even when I found women and other gender nonconforming people to be more interesting and alluring, I never knew what was supposed to happen next. I didn't know how to start the conversation with the rest of the people in my life. Dressing up for the male gaze was easy, so I kept those other desires shelved and my head in the hetero game.

But I couldn't shake the hyperawareness that there was very little room for me on the board. I noticed how much easier it was for some of my homegirls to thrive. Navigating the dating landscape just came natural to them, whereas it was a source of frustration and resistance for me. This difference between them and me was palpable and marked my earliest moments of identifying as "other." The moment I became sexually active, I came up against the stigma associated with sexuality and fat Black bodies. Like shaking ass for money, or throwing money to see it, attraction to fat girls has always been considered abnormal and a snub to those Western sexual scripts. Even now, the fact that my sex life has been so diverse and robust is sometimes mind-blowing to people. They react to this information as if I've outed myself as someone who fucks outside the realm of acceptability. In other words, way before I was having sex and relationships with people who were not cisgender men, I was queer.

In high school, having a bunch of close friends who were both embracing and struggling with their sexualities finally made me comfortable enough to even talk about also liking girls. I was slowly starting to put it together that if I didn't have to be hourglass shaped, super respectable, or sexually pure to be a baddie, I also didn't have to be straight. But I was straddling the fence, still clinging to my heterosexuality by playing up the fact that lesbianism was being fetishized by men. This was the era when Young Dro announced to the world that his "girl got a girlfriend." I was still fucking cis niggas,

Attn Gen Z readers:

Handwritten notes were once the primary means of communication amongst high schoolers. Even if some of us had cell phones, our network providers charged us extra for each text sent, and our parents could see them. So to ensure our privacy, we would write letters and fold them into unique designs before passing them along.

and I hadn't pursued or been pursued by any women. I wouldn't date or sleep with a woman until college, and I have AOL Instant Messenger (AIM) to thank for that.

Before we had our pick of social media outlets, and Facebook wasn't the shady enigma that it is today, AIM was that girl. It was an especially useful platform for a college student who was always on her laptop, anyway. During my sophomore year of college, I was using it primarily to keep in touch with one particular friend from high school. We'd known each other for a really long time, and she had come out to me in class, via one of the many handwritten letters we exchanged. She'd admitted that the mysterious guy from her waitressing job whom she'd been dating was actually a girl. In hindsight, that's such a classic Libra thing: building someone's trust while also lying to them. But I was supportive, even if I was a little caught off guard. We kept sharing notes, even more so now that the truth was out, and remained friends.

One day, as we chatted from different universities hundreds of miles away from each other, I had the sudden realization that Libra Bae was flirting with me. I was flattered, so I flirted back. For months we carried on like this over AIM, falling deeper for each other as time went on. Because we lived in different cities, we only got to see each other a couple of times a year, when we were both in town for the holidays. I would usually hang out with her and her family at their house. Or we'd all go to the movies or the bowling alley, but no one knew the nature of our relationship. To date, it's the most wholesome situationship

I've ever been in. The most we ever did was phone bone and kiss deeply in her car. Other than that, she'd sneak and hold my hand in the movies or privately graze my back when she knew no one was watching. Her family was super religious and she was deeply closeted. So we hung out together under the guise of being friends and never committed to actually being together. But we fantasized about it, a lot.

We carried on in that precarious "What are we?" phase for about six years, on and off. During our high periods, we spoke every single day, sharing I love yous and talking about the partners we would be to each other if things were different: if she reconciled her sexuality and her faith; if we lived in the same city or state; once we both got our shit together. There is no doubt in my mind that we had deep feelings for each other. I can say for sure that I was deeply in love with her. But Libra Bae was also full of shit, and after a while it became clear to me that she had no intention of seeing any of those promises to fruition, and not just because she wasn't out to her family.

We had different values and politics. Because of her upbringing, she was surprisingly conservative, at times making me feel like I was dating a gay Republican. Even though we were never monogamous (one thing about me is: we can't even start to have a conversation about me putting my pussy on ice if we're not in a committed relationship—I'll explain why in the relationship chapter) and we talked about other people she dated, she didn't like the idea of me fucking and dating other people. She hated that I was doing sex work. She was also low-key fat phobic. I figured that last part out later when I realized she was having plenty of sex with some of the other girls she dated, none of whom were fat, but not me.

It was never going to work out between Libra Bae and me. It was an emotional affair that never materialized in any real way. One time a homegirl straight-up asked me, "Does she really exist?" because none of my friends who didn't already know her from our high school had actually met her. Over the course of our time together, there was never any effort put forth to visit or fly me to her. Still, she was a come up from all of the raggedy niggas I was fucking with over the course of the years when we talked. She was the first person to take me on a date. She helped me out with money when I needed it. She helped me realize how I deserved and wanted to be treated by partners, and I'll always be grateful to her for that. But she also taught me my first lesson in not dating people who aren't out.

Libra Bae cussed me out and blocked me when I told her that I'd met Violet, the person who would become my first real girlfriend. They actually had quite a bit in common—they were both fine as hell; they both had strong, faith-based backgrounds; and neither of them lived in the same city as me. But they were different in one super-important aspect: Violet didn't have any reservations about us or our relationship. We dated, publicly, and spent meaningful time together. We had mutual friends, and I loved when we all kicked it because it gave me an opportunity to get to know Violet's character. She wasn't just letting me see one side of her because she was my secret lover. I could vouch for her sincerity and integrity, and I never had doubts about how she felt about me. We dated for a few months and then she asked me to be her girlfriend. It was that simple. The partnership I'd dreamt about with Libra Bae became a reality with Violet.

Because we were in a long-distance relationship in which she mostly came to visit me, I didn't know that Violet wasn't "out" to her friends and family back home. I knew she often presented super femme for work and church, and she would rock joggers and Jordans with a full face beat. I loved her fluidity and her androgynous style, but she still oozed big dyke energy. No amount of foundation, lipstick, or pencil skirts could hide that. When I found out that she was keeping her sexuality a secret, my first thought was *How could they not know?!* But even if I didn't understand how Violet kept her sexuality a secret, I knew why she did. She was extremely close with her family. They lived together and worked in similar spaces. Christianity was a huge part of their lives, and they were not the open-minded Christians who made room for gay folks. Violet wasn't just worried about facing her family's disappointment or shame. To live as she truly wanted meant risking her entire community, her housing, and her livelihood. There was a lot at stake, and she wasn't ready to chance it.

Since we had mostly spent time in my city and with my people, I didn't fully understand how much of a barrier this would be for us. Violet effortlessly stepped into my world and we were happy in it. But my first trip to visit her hometown proved that stepping into hers wouldn't be as easy. She was afraid to hold my hand or be affectionate with me in public for fear of members of her church seeing us. I got to meet her family, but like Libra Bae, we were forced to do so under the guise of friendship. It was tense and not at all how I wanted my life to be in partnership with someone. It was difficult to think about what our relationship would look like as I stepped into the next phase of my life and career. Violet couldn't offer a lot of answers on that front yet. To move forward in the ways I needed her to would have meant she had to leave some things behind, and she wasn't ready to do that. I also wanted to see other people and she didn't. So we decided to end our relationship.

These days I choose to date queer folks who have already crossed the bridge of shame and potential backlash that comes with opening up about their love life. It's not because I can't support someone who is struggling through that process but because it's too much to ask of someone who isn't ready. It's not easy to walk away from the life you have just to pursue your sexual and romantic desires, and it's not an experience that you walk away from unscathed.

I know this because my current, primary partner—my Genius Bae—actually did it. Over a decade before she met me, she made a conscious decision to walk away from the environment of religious extremism she was raised in. As a result, she lost contact with her parents, her childhood friends, and a robust support system. She swapped out the pressure to conform to their way of life for the weight of guilt she carries for doing so. I love her through these internal conflicts and watch helplessly as she still struggles to build new connections. It's harder to let people in when you understand how easily even the strongest bonds can be broken. I would take her pain away from her if I could. But it's also the only way she and I get to have the life we enjoy together. I don't take any of it lightly.

"Coming out" isn't part of my queer identity or story, but not because I decided against making a hoopla about the fact that I liked bitches. It's because, unlike Libra Bae, Violet, and Genius Bae, I didn't have as much to lose. I got older and realized that the stuff my straight friends have to deal with when dating men feels really silly to me. I liked that I didn't have to follow as many rules about who I was supposed to be when I was with women. I also didn't have to "come out," because as a cisgender femme, my gender expression doesn't put a target on my back when I walk out the door. It does not pose a threat to the gender binary or hierarchy. Last but not least, I didn't have to "come out" at the risk of alienating myself from my loved ones. I come from a Christian family too. I'm sure they would love nothing more than for me to be laid up under a successful husband and carrying his child right now. But my family mostly believes in independence and minding their own business. Whatever adjustments they had to make to accommodate the fact that I suddenly had female partners were made without my knowledge. They've found ways to love and accept me and my partner, despite their own beliefs. They've held me down and I'm grateful for that.

I wish more Black queer and trans people were held like this. Let's have more Black mamas willing to love their gay and trans sons and daughters through whatever, and willing to die before they let a nigga make their child feel unwelcome in their home. Let's have more Black women willing to check her homegirls about their homophobia. Let's have more Black mamas bring their girlfriends home and take their daughters to Pride picnics. Let's have more grandmas who don't give a damn that their granddaughter walks in the crib "lookin' like a lil boy" and just wants to make sure she eats.

My biggest beef with the heterosexual narrative (not to be confused with people who are heterosexual) is that it pulls us away from this type of communal support. It requires that Black women instead participate in transphobia and homophobia. It asks that Black women look the other way when it comes to the abuse that cishet men perpetuate against them and members of the queer community, for the sake of Black "family." It asks everyone to put a cap on their sexual desire, expression, and identity. It requires a scarcity mindset as opposed to an abundant one, which is exactly why my homegirl Amber J. Phillips calls heterosexuality "the ghetto." It's the only ghetto I want no part of.

Chapter 8

FUCK THESE NIGGAS

I don't want this nigga. Baby, spare me the drama.

—Saucy Santana, "Boy Damn"[1]

Frederick Douglass's first wife, Anna Murray Douglass, was a free Black woman when they met and married. Her status kept him inspired to pursue his own freedom, and Anna encouraged him. She took some sailor's clothing from her job so that he could have a disguise, gave him some of the money she'd saved up, and sent him north so that he, too, could be relieved from the bondage of slavery. She joined him shortly after and helped set up their household when they settled in Massachusetts. She worked to support the family and their ongoing efforts to help other Black folks escape slavery. Fred's glow up as a free man continued as he became a preacher, a prominent abolitionist, then bestselling author once he penned an autobiography. Suddenly he was traveling the world and rubbing elbows with notable socialites and intellectuals of the time, leaving Anna behind at home. The rumors of Fred's infidelity started circulating not long after. He was suspected of having affairs with at least a couple of white women; one of whom would even live with him and Anna for a couple of months at a time. Despite the role she played in him becoming a prominent figure in Black and American history, Anna is hardly mentioned in any of Fred's autobiographical works. A year after she died, this nigga Fred married Helen Pitts, a white woman who was their neighbor and his employee.

When Harriet Tubman escaped from slavery in Dorchester County, Maryland, in 1849, she was married to John Tubman. But she left him behind in her own pursuit of freedom. Like Anna Murray Douglass, John was a free Black man. However, unlike Anna, John wasn't super supportive of his wife's plan to liberate herself. Clearly Harriet didn't let that stop her from escaping to Philadelphia; nor did her husband's opinion stop her from making several trips back to their home state in order to free other enslaved family members. On one of those trips in 1851, she planned to find John and bring him back to Philadelphia with her. She even bought him a new suit for the journey. When she sent word to clue him in on her plan, he said no. That nigga John had married another woman named Caroline while Harriet was liberating their people. He said he was happy exactly where he was.

The stories of Harriet Tubman and Frederick Douglass are vital to Black history. They tell of our struggles, our resilience, and our victories. But a closer look at the love lives of our ancestors offers historical anecdotes that support another, important, underlying fact: when it comes to dating and relationships, these niggas ain't shit. Black women often receive the short end of the stick. It would be irresponsible of me to share any perspectives on romantic relationships and not make that clear up front.

I would like to make a quick point of clarification, though. In the context of dating, I tend to use "niggas" as a gender-neutral term that includes cis men, studs, and transmasculine folks who primarily date femmes. You can apply a lot of what I'm going to say in this chapter to whomever you date, across the gender spectrum. But I think a trap feminist dating framework is especially pertinent if you're dating cis men. Why? Because cis men have set the tone for the toxicity that some of their queer and trans peers embody. Them niggas are the source of a lot of this shit. Toxic masculinity is not simply a heinous trait that only certain men develop because of their trauma or upbringing. The very concept of Western masculinity is inherently toxic because it's built on the premise of domination and control. It gives cisgender, heterosexual men—and sometimes other folks who identify with and perform "acceptable" masculinity—ample opportunity to participate in this toxicity, and they choose to do so because it benefits them. Because toxic masculinity has been so normalized and institutionalized, showing up in everything from healthcare to the justice system, the likelihood that men will face any backlash or consequences is low. This is especially true when their harmfulness is directed toward Black women.

In 2020, Blackburn Center (an anti-violence organization based in Greensburg, Pennsylvania) published a report noting that over 52 percent of all Black women had experienced psychological abuse and over 41 percent had experienced physical abuse. The report also documented that Black women are nearly three times as likely to die at the hands of a man than white women are. The report was even more specific about who was perpetuating these violations: "In the overwhelming majority of these cases—92%—the person who killed them knew their victim. 56% of these homicides were committed by a current or former intimate partner. Nearly all—92%—of these killings were intra-racial, which means that they were committed by a Black man against a Black woman."[2]

Black women are uniquely exposed to these worst-case outcomes. We have not been immune to the impact of anti-Black racism and state-sanctioned violence. We can't trust government officials or programs to act in our best interests, and we don't want to create more opportunities for members of our community to be harmed by the US penal system. In our efforts to prevent more harm from coming to ourselves, our children, and other loved ones, we end up protecting Black men who've hurt us. This is what happened to Megan Thee Stallion when she was shot by fellow artist Tory Lanez in 2020. On the night of the incident she wouldn't tell the police or medical professionals how she came by her injuries. She refused to share details of the crime, or even name her perpetrator, for over a month for fear that it would have made a bad situation even worse. When she finally did name Tory as her shooter, she was met with silence from her industry peers, and doubt from internet trolls.

Beyond the way that Black women are expected to protect Black men for the good of the culture is something even more insidious. We're also expected to overlook their faults, even be willing to accept those faults, for the sake of their affections. We're actually asked to take responsibility for all the ways niggas can be trash. Consider the way Black single mothers, the parents who take on the majority of the responsibility for their children, are ostracized and often blamed for all the ills of the Black community. Their parenting skills and judgment are called into question. They're mocked and written off as unintelligent and amoral. Whenever they're celebrated for being beautiful, happy, successful, or rich, there is always someone rushing to claim that the "baby mama lifestyle" is being "glorified."

Black women are written off as bitter and divisive if they publicly acknowledge the widespread sexism in Black communities, or share their own experiences with toxic masculinity, as reasons for caution or hesitation in dating. They're asked to question their own attributes and the decisions that prevented them from having better experiences. Were they beautiful, strong, submissive, freaky, pious, or respectable enough? Were they forgiving enough? Were they raised by one of those single mothers? If only Black women played their cards right, their true king would present himself. #BlackLove can prevail as long as Black women play their parts.

Unfortunately, a lot of Black women have bought right into this bullshit. I know way too many Black women for whom "That's why you still single" is an insult of the highest degree. They fall into depression and feel like failures because they're not tethered romantically to someone. On the flip side, I know way too many

Black women who think having and being able to "keep" a man is a flex, even when said man is broke, unreliable, unfaithful, or trifling. Pick Me Twitter is a real place where you can watch Black women pledge their allegiance to men with subtle brags about how much they're willing to cook, clean, fuck, and stay loyal to men who publicly shame the women they think are out of line. They've drunk the Kool-Aid and love the taste of it.

Black women have been gaslit into believing in a version of love that requires us to, first and foremost, de-center ourselves. Our love has been equated with a form of martyrdom; it grows stronger the more we suffer and hold niggas down, and somehow that's supposed to be good for all of us. I'm here to tell you: that ain't it, sis. The narrative Beyoncé offered us in *Lemonade*, that on the other side of the worst betrayal of your life is redemption that will make it all worth it, should not be a blueprint for relationships. If anything it was an epic fantasy saga created by a woman worth nearly half a billion dollars, married to a man worth even more. I love Bey and her genius, and I'm happy that she got the happily ever after *she* wanted. But do not fall for the okeydoke. Waiting two decades for your man to go to therapy so he can properly prioritize you as his partner is just not a good idea.

Black women can no longer afford to be martyrs, healers, parents, or scapegoats in our relationships. It's a fucking scam. The stakes are too high. It's costing us our sanity, our livelihoods, and in some cases our lives. If you experienced a string of break-ins in your neighborhood, would you still leave

your doors and windows unlocked, just because your property manager or HOA president promised the neighborhood
was safe when you moved in? No. So don't ignore the realities
of intimate-partner violence, romantic terrorism, and all the
other ways niggas generally "ain't shit," or assume that you'll
somehow be the exception to the rule. Accept that they are the
way they are and act accordingly.

*　　*　　*

I knew there was hope for us after the Hot Girl Summer of
2019. Taking their name from one of Megan Thee Stallion's mon-
ikers, Hot Girls ran the streets right alongside their City Girl
counterparts. No one's nigga was safe. Stories of their partying,
dating around, gladly taking men's money, and reveling in the
pleasure they got from their debauchery captured the minds and
hearts of the masses. Their conquests were tagged—sometimes
literally using hashtags, but often colloquially—with labels like
"real hot girl shit" and "city girls up 10 points." They refused to
play by the rules of modesty and courtesy, refused to perform a
version of traditionally acceptable Black femininity, and refused
to take any L's. They were de-centering men and romantic relationships from their zeitgeists, and winning, while the world
watched. Brands and corporations sought to capitalize off Hot
Girl Summer as a sticky catchphrase, without understanding its
real implications. A blueprint was being drawn that could actually liberate a generation of Black women who might otherwise

play themselves. A trap feminist model for dating went viral, and I couldn't have been happier.

Of course, city girls didn't invent the "Fuck niggas, get money" model. Although, they have made excellent use of new technologies to expand its playing field. There have always been women who understood the game: The auntie that the rest of the women in your family whisper about, who's always traveling seemingly alone. The college classmate with the Louis Vuitton tote whom people call a hoe, even though they can't confidently name a single one of her bodies (sexual partners). The girl you suspect your nigga might be cheating with. The girl you used to work with who was juggling three dudes six months ago but just popped up on your Instagram feed, engaged. The women who were called hoes and mocked for being single but, when it came down to it, seemed a lot happier than the married women who talked shit about them.

They did exactly what the fuck they wanted to do and let the rest work itself out. These women had the cheat code. It's that boss bitch energy, with a sprinkle of scandal, that so many female rappers tap into in their songs and videos. So many of us assume that this version of reality is unattainable when we've actually been given a syllabus we could have been using this whole time. A new G Wagon might need to be worked into a five-year plan, but you can have a love life that benefits you, and not some nigga, this week.

Before we dive into that, though, I want to make it clear that there is nothing you can do to stop a nigga from cheating. There is nothing you can do to stop a nigga from being abusive. You can be the perfect woman, have the fattest ass, make the best mac and cheese, have great credit, and draw up a business plan that will help make your boo a millionaire. You can run background checks and sit in his mama's face for hours asking questions about his childhood and his exes to get to know him better. You can pray, meditate, and fast. None of it will stop a nigga from nig'ing if that's what the nigga wants to do. Nor is it your fault if he does. If a nigga is trash, that's on him. You don't have to take any of that on.

What I hope to make plain is how you can avoid being completely shattered if he is. I hope you feel empowered enough to see fuck shit sooner and swerve right around it. Make a full U-turn if you have to. I hope you're able to honor a version of Black womanhood that is not tangled up in whether or not you've locked down a commitment from someone. I hope you understand that not having a nigga at all is actually better than having a trash one. I'm going to share how I follow a trap feminist model in relationships, and how I fumbled when I didn't. Every single thing may not apply to you and your specific circumstances, but I promise you, this model hasn't let me down.

1. I take care of myself.

I tend to think of relationships and dating as a luxury, not a necessity. What's necessary is that my own proverbial house is in order. Once that groundwork is laid, then I've earned the right to splurge. My most successful relationships feel like cherries on top of an already good dessert. I'm satisfied in the same way I am when I execute a flawless face beat. I feel elevated and more beautiful, but I know that my skin, underneath it all, is still damn near perfect. My relationships fulfill me like a perfect chill weekend can refill my spirit. I look forward to them, I appreciate them, I bask in their glow, but I wouldn't be able to if it weren't for all that weekday grinding and showing up during the rest of the month. I like to make sure that I can afford, financially and emotionally, to date. The goal for me is to maintain a state of *I'll be okay, with or without this nigga.*

I've created a life for myself that I enjoy, and I feel absolutely no kind of way about not dating folks who don't fit into that lifestyle. I know what kinds of dates I like because I take myself on them. I have my own coin and take care of my own responsibilities, so I never have to worry about a nigga leaving me out on the street, using material things as a form of manipulation, or fucking up my credit. Prenups get a bad rep, but you can bet your ass I'm signing one if I ever get married. The sense of guaranteed financial security *if* we break up is worth more to me than a promise that we never will. A nigga can help me with my own financial goals, but it's my responsibility to make sure they can never hurt my pockets.

I cringe a little when I see my friends bragging about their sexual/romantic partners when they're also in a state of financial turmoil. I can't imagine a life for myself that would involve me entertaining multiple non-platonic relationships and still having to fundraise for my rent money. When I've been in relationships in which either my partner or myself was struggling financially, our partnership reflected that instability. We didn't go places, we didn't experience new things together, and we couldn't enjoy the present because we were so focused on figuring out what was next. If it's true that partners meet each other where they are, I was meeting people riding the same fucking struggle bus I was on when I was broke. Never again. I think everyone deserves love and intimacy, if that's what they want for themselves, but they have a responsibility to make sure they're in a place to ask that of someone else.

Taking care of myself isn't just limited to my financial responsibilities either. It also includes maintaining my confidence, my ambition, and my own identity. When I was trying to date while going through deep depressions or bouts of insecurity or self-hate, I couldn't get a grip on why I even wanted to be in a relationship, let alone how I should be treated in one. I followed Libra Bae into a cloud of elusiveness because I lacked clarity in my own life. I didn't know where I was headed, so every idea she had about our future sounded like a good one. Even if I didn't know it at that time, I didn't have the mental or emotional capacity to try to build a life with someone. As my emotional well-being improved (I literally moved to a new city, started graduate school, got my finances in order, and started to overcome some major mental health hurdles over the course of my fake relationship with Libra Bae), I was finally able to make sense of what was really happening with us. I suddenly saw the smoke and mirrors. Now that I've done that work, my character can't be compromised. I know my boundaries, I know my standards, and I know how to communicate them to anyone who wants to deal with me.

One of the biggest mistakes anyone can make in dating is to go in unprepared or unfulfilled. Desperation and discontent cloud your judgment and perspective, especially when it comes to people you're still getting to know. These deficits make it harder to tell whether or not the relationship is working, whether the person is worth your time, and if your needs are being met. If you're not taking care of yourself, how do you know what care looks like? If your relationship with this other person dictates the person you are, then whose life are you really living? A partner can add value to my life in a lot of ways, but they cannot take anything away from it. My primary commitment is always to myself, because I can't show up for anyone else if my shit is not together.

Let's go back to our good sis Harriet Tubman real quick and look at what happened after she realized John Tubman was a dub. She was obviously pissed and hurt about it, but she didn't make a scene. She got right back to work, and instead of escorting her now ex-husband to Pennsylvania, she led another group of enslaved Black folks to freedom. She became the visionary we're still honoring over a hundred years after her death. She also remarried: Nelson Charles Davis, a veteran and bricklayer who was twenty-two years younger than her. They were together for nineteen years before he died of tuberculosis. Despite the work she did on behalf of her people and this raggedy ass country, Harriet experienced a lot of financial hardship later in life. This isn't because she wasn't a boss; it's because she was a Black woman in nineteenth-century America. What matters is that she never lost sight of her goals and purpose, and she didn't rush to be someone else's wife. I like to think that before she remarried she had a boo or two who caught her eye and kept her company, and my hope is that during her marriage to Nelson she was getting her back properly blown out. I like to imagine that she was happy, fulfilled, and just fucking fine without John. Why? Because she knew who she was and her shit was together.

2. I only date people who take care of themselves.

When Michelle Obama said she was only willing to date Barack because he was already a "fully formed" person, I felt that in my spirit. I was equally moved when the prophetesses known as City Girls proclaimed that "broke niggas don't deserve no pussy." As far as I'm concerned, these are two sides of the same coin. I can't date anyone who doesn't have their shit together, and I can promise you that they won't be getting any coochie from me.

If you've made it this far in the book, then you understand

all the circumstances I've had to overcome and all the work I've had to do to be a bad bitch. I need that exact same energy from my boo. I want to know that you're managing your finances, taking care of your responsibilities, staying true to who you are, and moving toward who you want to be. Furthermore, the love languages that I am most receptive to are gifts and acts of service. I like to be spoiled and worshipped by my lovers. I want to date someone I can have exciting, new experiences with. You need a discretionary budget to date a bitch like me. I am very understanding of the realities of capitalism, economic inequality, and class warfare. I've lived through many of them. I empathize with those in the struggle, but at this point in my life, I can't join you in that struggle. I'm not passing judgment, but I'm not going to fuck you. It doesn't matter how much chemistry we have or how well we get along.

One of my Tinder matches had to learn this the hard way. We'd been chatting for a couple of weeks, and one day he offered to pick me up from dinner with a friend. It was cold as hell in New York that night, and I really didn't want to take the subway home, so I welcomed this particular act of service. I'd already verified his identity, and my friend was able to get his license plate number, so I felt safe when he scooped me in his little hoopty. We chatted all the way to Brooklyn in a revealing conversation that led me to the conclusion that I absolutely did *not* want to date him. He was a cool guy and we got along great. But he was broke as hell and basically told me as much. When I told him that I liked to travel, he proposed we plan a road trip in his hoopty to cut down on the cost of flights. He also told me he had a kid and was struggling to make his child support payments. He was hoping his child's mother would agree to reduce the payments since she'd just gotten a new job.

This is no shade to him. He didn't strike me as a deadbeat dad, just a broke one. I also have no doubt that there are plenty of women out there who would gladly date him. I just wasn't one of those women. It would have gone against everything I believe in to date someone who has to scrape together money to buy me a proper birthday gift, or use a weekend he should have been spending with his kid to take me on a trip. The way my feminism is set up, I don't want to be the reason another Black woman is shortchanged on the resources she needs to raise her children.

I allowed myself to enjoy our conversation and I smoked the blunt he'd rolled for us. I felt very much like I was talking to one of my guy friends from back home. We laughed and kiki'd until I was ready to go home. There was no flirting, kissing, or anything like that on my part. When he texted me the next morning, I made it clear that I just wanted to be friends. I was surprised when he responded like this:

Him: *I feel like you're saying that because of my financial situation and that if I could do the things you were interested in doing, you'd feel differently.*

Me: *That's correct.*

Him: *That's fair. I just need a chance to adjust instead of being ruled out before you find out you're in love.*

I stood my ground, and he ended up sending me the word "compromise" in all caps, and misspelled. I'd only met him once, we were on the same page that he didn't fit what I was looking for in a lover, and he *still* thought the possibility of fALLiNg iN lOvE would convince me to reconsider my own standards. He thought I should be willing after our knowing each other for twelve hours. He thought wrong, obviously.

But I tell that story because: one, niggas will try you, every time; two, love, by itself, isn't enough to sustain a relationship if both parties aren't taking care of themselves or each other. Black women are often shamed for not wanting to take on other people's baggage, for not being the bigger person, for not seeing the potential of the people who like them, for not being willing to do some work up front. I'm not a therapist, a business mentor, a life coach, or a crisis manager. Those are hats I often have to wear in my own life or pay someone else to take on for me. I am not taking on any of those roles to date someone. I want a lover, not a job. I refuse to feel bad about it either.

3. I live and date by my own morals and principles, and no one else's.

Among the first words I ever heard Trina speak were "I ain't ashamed of nothing I do." I've taken that shit to heart. For every standard a Black woman sets for herself, there is a negative spin that can and has been put on it. If she refuses to date broke, she's a gold digger. If she does date broke, she's a sucker. If she's not dating seriously, she's a hoe. If she is dating seriously, she hasn't succeeded until she gets the ring. If she doesn't want to be married, she's lying or damaged. If she has an abortion, she's a monster. If she has kids out of wedlock, she's a tired baby mama. The reasons and methods used to shame Black women for their choices in sex, dating, and relationships are endless. We're damned if we do and damned if we don't. That's why I use my own moral compass to do what works for me.

A lot of my dating philosophies fall outside what is considered acceptable. For some people, my refusal to date people who have children under a certain age or don't have enough disposable income means I'm materialistic and self-centered. They're entitled to that opinion, but it won't make me suddenly available to broke niggas with kids.

I'm also ethically nonmonogamous. I like having a primary partner and the option to date and have sex with other people if I want to. That suits me and my inner hoochie. This setup also works for my partner, who has the same freedom. We love each other very deeply and are very grateful that we've continued to choose each other. But our genuine happiness with each other does not stop people who think that monogamy is the foundation of all healthy relationships from questioning and doubting our choice. "Why be in a relationship if you still want to fuck other people?" "What if you decide you want to be serious?" "I could never . . ." As if I asked them.

One of the unfortunate outcomes of Black women continuously de-centering themselves in relationships is that they learn to rely on a set of scripts and narratives about what love should look like. There isn't a lot of room for them to figure out what their own individual needs are. There is no single model of relationships that works for every partnership. You actually have to try out a few different configurations, with either the same or different partners, to figure out what works for you. This is why the "hoe phase" is so important. You should know what all your options are before settling. But even dating multiple people is subject to scrutiny.

To that I'll offer two pieces of insight: One, I have never met a woman who regretted her hoe phase, lifestyle, and/or identity. However, I've met several women who are married, or out of the game for other reasons, who feel like they missed out and deeply regret not having a hoe phase. Two, I've never met a hoe who couldn't transition into a housewife with the right person.

People will try to find a reason to devalue you whether you've fucked five people or fifty. Keep it cute. Keep it low-key. Take care of yourself. Keep it a buck with yourself and do what you want.

4. I set the tone.

I met Baller when I was eighteen. He was a few years older than me, and it should be noted that his alias has nothing to do with his income. We'd only ever hung out in group settings

keep it a buck:

At some point, keeping it real morphed into keeping it one hundred. A dollar, which is one hundred cents, is also called a buck. After wealthy designer Virgil Abloh bragged about donating fifty dollars to the Black Lives Matter movement in 2020, people began to use the phrase "Keep it two Virgils."

with mutual friends until one day when we were alone and he shot his shot. His interest caught me completely off guard, and it wasn't a romantic proposition by any stretch of the imagination. He'd been thinking about fucking me and he wanted to know if I'd be down. That was the pitch. Luckily for him, I wasn't looking for romance, and I was curious. So we went back to his place, took a few shots of cheap vodka, and commenced a sexual fling that lasted for the better part of a decade.

Midday quickies were our thing for a while, with the occasional late-night romp thrown in. We kept it mostly between ourselves so it wouldn't be weird when we hung out with our friends. When I found out he had a girlfriend, my feelings weren't hurt. But I noticed it wasn't something he was up front about. We carried on. Things became more adventurous for us as we involved other people in our antics and took our talents on the road. We linked at different spots, in a couple of different cities. When he found himself in the middle of some dust between me and one of my best friends, I played it cool with him. We weren't serious and there were no strings attached. We carried on. Eventually I moved to the East Coast, and we kept in touch via Gchat. We'd fall in and out of touch depending on what our other relationships required. He got married. I moved again, twice. We carried on. Six years had gone by.

While we certainly were not on the path to any relationship, Baller and I had moved beyond the point of "no strings attached." There were strings; they were just really fucking raggedy. Besides some fairly consistent orgasms, a lot of regular degular weed, and a few shits and giggles, I had nothing to show for our little fling. I'd never received a single gift; he'd never offered a helping hand or even a morsel of advice or inspiration that has stuck with me. The only meaningful impact he had on my life was completely changing the relationship I had with one of my best friends, and he somehow managed to wash his hands of the situation. Baller never bothered himself with the details of my life. My successes and my failures were met with the same lack of enthusiasm.

I mirrored that energy and played my part. I wasn't looking for anything serious, and ethically I had nothing against casual sex or friends with benefits. Because there were no expectations in place, Baller couldn't have broken any rules or crossed any boundaries. I didn't think I had a right to suddenly feel unfulfilled and undervalued after all of these years, and I knew he would be dismissive if I brought it up. His idea of a resolution was that I got to a place where I was still willing to deepthroat him the next time we linked. When I didn't want to be bothered anymore, I knew I didn't have to give a reason why. So I fell back, always offering some vague, personal reason for the sudden unavailability of my vagina. But secretly I felt a resentment toward him that I didn't even understand at the time.

So much about me and how I engaged with lovers had changed in the years since I'd met Baller as an eighteen-year-old. I'd had different kinds of relationships and friends with benefits, connections that were serving me in different ways. At first I wrote my lingering, negative feelings toward him off as righteous anger at the fact that he was only ever interested in the "benefits" but never true friendship with me. His priority was always whether or not this pussy was available to him; everything else was white noise. He didn't appreciate the bad bitch I'd become, right in front of his face. I thought that was his bad, but then I realized it was actually mine.

He never offered or gave me anything because I'd never asked. He never gave a fuck how I felt about things, but I never made that a requirement. I'd set a tone for us, and he got in where he fit in. He played the role he was always going to play, and I let him. All that resentment I felt wasn't because he'd played me; it was because I'd played myself. Toward the end, our fling became a reflection of who I was when I was at my worst. The only reason Baller and I hooked up in the first place is because I didn't have the standards I have now. But he was clear from the day we met who he was, what he wanted, and what he was willing to offer. I said okay and, in doing so, sealed my own fate.

People can change, but you can't change people. Don't ever let your ego convince you otherwise. People are going to do what they want to do, but in most cases, they can only do to you what you allow them to do. These days, I make it clear what I want and need from all of my partners up front. When I met Genius Bae, I literally sent her a list after she slid into my DMs, trying to shoot her shot: I told her I needed to be able to ask for things I wanted and needed. I told her I expected a lot of privacy, and a lot of head. I told her she needed to have a sense of humor (turns out she's a huge comedy fan). I was half joking, but all she said was: "I can do that." There have been folks who've balked at these needs, and that's okay because being clear helps weed those motherfuckers out before they waste any of my time. It's a win-win.

5. Words and labels mean things, so I use them wisely.

Maybe it's because I'm a Capricorn and I love having clarity and understanding, but I am *not* one of those people who think that labels complicate things. I think that labels help set boundaries and can offer a guiding light for where a situation is headed. Whenever I hear people, especially Black women, express their apprehension about labels in their love lives, I always assume: she is dealing with someone who already isn't meeting her expectations; she doesn't trust the person; or she's also dealing with other people she's not ready to cut off. In my experience, labels don't complicate things, people do. But labels do change things because of what they mean.

I can fuck someone and not be dating them; I can be dating someone, but that doesn't mean they're my partner. Part of how I set the tone in my relationships is that I don't pretend we're something that we're not. I'm always clear on "what we are" so that I can act accordingly. I don't go out in public or share too many personal details with people I'm just fucking.

I don't cook and clean or have sleepovers for more than a few days with folks unless I'm their girlfriend. I don't play house, let my time be dictated, or feel the need to stop dating other people (if they prefer monogamy) with folks who are not my partner. If I think I want to move from one stage to another with someone, I'm up front about it. If we're on the same page, we talk about expectations and what a reconfiguration might look like. If not, I fall back. I love those lines drawn in the sand.

What matters most is that I'm clear on what these labels mean to *me* and how each of them could possibly serve me. For example, even though I know I'm not necessarily the marrying kind, I definitely believe in sacred bonds between lovers who've chosen to build a life together. I think there is value in commitment, even if I've never felt strongly about the institution of marriage. However, I don't put every person I date on a track to be my life partner, because everything isn't for everyone. And if they want to be on that path with me, I need to trust that they can fulfill that role in my life. The first rule of both hoeing and trapping is to get the money first. I keep this same energy around dating and relationships. I make them put up or shut up.

6. I know when to walk away.

You know those funny memes about taking your nigga back for the thirty-seventh time and being a clown for him? I hate them. One thing about me is: I'll cut a nigga off real quick. I truly believe that I'm *that* bitch and access to me is a privilege. You earn it by treating me well and adding value to my life. If that's not what you're doing, why are you here? It's really that simple for me. I don't have to justify my standards or prove myself because I know who I am. Act right or see yourself out.

If this is something you struggle with, here is one more anecdote: It's also been my experience that after you walk away (and sometimes after they walk away) these niggas *always* come back. It might not be today, it might not be next week, it might be a year from now, but eventually you'll get that "Hey, stranger" or "I miss my friend" text. So don't ever sweat your decision to walk away from a situation that doesn't serve you. You're not losing out on anything, and you can always change your mind later. You are the prize and you are the priority. Fuck these niggas.

Chapter 9

MY BITCHES

She gon' ride till the wheels fall off.

—Dreezy, "We Gon' Ride"[1]

There's one other rule I follow when I'm dating: I don't date people who don't take friendship seriously. It's a huge red flag. Anyone who wants to date me but doesn't want me to have any platonic friends is more than likely super controlling, possessive, and abusive. These kinds of people want to keep you isolated from your support system and anyone else who won't sit idly by while they terrorize you. At best, a partner requires too much of my time if they think our romantic relationship shouldn't leave me with any time to be in community with my bitches. I don't even entertain the problematic rhetoric that a relationship is only healthy if my friends are kept squarely outside of it. I understand why people say that. They think that just because you might forgive your partner doesn't mean that your friends and family will forgive them if they know what the person has done, and that there will always be tension. But that "no friends" shit still doesn't work for me. See, the way my friendships are set up, I know my friends are going to support me and my decisions, even if they don't agree with them. They don't have to fuck my partner, I do.

Plus, having space to process my relationship is way more important to me than my partner feeling nervous that my friends don't like them. My homegirls give me that. They are my counsel. I don't need the gang to support my boo or my relationship; I need them to support *me*. These are going to be the women who will help me rob you if you fuck up, no matter how friendly they act when you're around, so don't get too excited for their approval.

On the flip side, I'm also completely uninterested in dating anyone who doesn't have any friends themselves. The last guy I was in a relationship with was a serial monogamist (except he wasn't monogamous). When I met him, Levi was living with his then-serious girlfriend. They broke up, he moved back in with his parents, and we were officially a couple a few weeks after. While he had plenty of stories about his exes and old fuck buddies, I didn't know him to have a single homeboy, or homegirl for that matter. This detail slipped right on by me in the first few months of our relationship. But eventually I saw how our lifestyles weren't balancing out. When I wasn't with him, or at school or work, I was with my homegirls. I would reference them in conversations with him and he'd met most of them. But I was getting none of that energy back from him.

So one day I had to straight-up ask him, "Do you have any friends? I'd like to meet them." He stared at me blankly. I could tell my inquiry had surprised him. He clearly hadn't considered

I might have been factoring his friendships into his personality profile. But the fact that he didn't really have an answer for me also threw him off. He thought about it for half a second more and then stammered something about a girl named Letitia. He said they'd recently met at the community college where he was taking classes. I told him I looked forward to meeting her and left it at that.

Unfortunately, that meeting never came to fruition. Not long after I confronted him about his lack of a social life, we got into a serious argument about what he had planned for the rest of his life. I was busting my ass to get to class and work every day because I had a graduation and a move to Washington, DC, looming in the near future. Meanwhile, I kept having to nag him about keeping basic ass food service jobs, even if he didn't feel "passionately" about them. Apparently this was too much pressure for him, and my staunch opposition to his lack of ambition made him feel "attacked." He threw in the towel. In a moment of weakness and stupidity on my part a couple of weeks later, I reached out to him, hoping we could figure things out and possibly move forward. But Levi declined. He was done with our relationship. Him and Letitia were together now, and he wanted to try to make things work with her. Apparently, she was more accepting of his lifestyle.

I wasn't mad that Levi was dating someone else, especially since our relationship was open. But I was livid that he'd planned on introducing this bitch to me as his platonic friend. To this day, he insists that when he told me about Letitia, they really were just friends, which is missing the point. Him and Letitia were able to slip into a romantic relationship so quickly after we broke up because to Levi, a "friend" is just someone he hasn't fucked yet. Because he didn't comprehend the meaning of friendship, he didn't understand why I felt so disrespected by this turn of events. Levi was a relationship guy. Fresh romantic energy lit him up and kept him going. But every last one of his girlfriends had to deal with the foundation that was missing because he didn't have any friends.

Levi just wasn't equipped to deal with life. He had daddy issues. He was unmotivated. Despite being super creative and passionate about justice and equity (qualities that had drawn me to him), he didn't have any vision for his life. He saw himself purely through the eyes of the women he dated. I always wondered how much of that would have been different if he'd had more intentional, platonic friendships that inspired him. How might he have understood his place in the world differently if he had to show up for someone who expected nothing of him but to be himself? How would he have navigated our relationship, and his life, differently if he had some homies he wasn't interested in fucking?

There isn't anything wrong with being in romantic love and enjoying the experience of it. However, in my experience, people tend to do better in relationships when they have at least one solid platonic friendship. Friendship connects us to ourselves in a way that we take for granted. Our friendships tend to exist outside the power dynamics that govern so many of our other relationships. Your parents demand a certain reverence. You're tied to your siblings and cousins by blood. Professional interests and ambition connect you to mentors. You may share children, vows, a legal union, living expenses, and/or desire with your boo. (If you don't already share those things, you're likely considering how those things fit into the future that y'all are trying to build together.) Friendship, though? It requires nothing more than an ongoing decision to love each other.

Too many people mistake the unprescribed nature of friendships to mean they are disposable, when the opposite is true. Friendship is one of the purest forms of love precisely because you love your friends voluntarily. The payoff, having someone who loves you back, just because, is also greater. The vulnerability that each party brings to equitable friendships is unmatched. Friendship is how you get really good practice in empathy, healthy conflict resolution, and how to build and be in community. It's how you learn to appreciate community so that you're not headed into your other relationships expecting one person to be your everything. Real friends will call you out on your bullshit as many times as necessary. Friendship allows for more checks and balances in your romantic relationship because, ideally, you both have people in your individual corners to have your back and hold you accountable at the same time. Yes, my friends know my business, and I wouldn't have it any other way. Friendships keep us safe.

We live in a society that has prioritized romantic and familial relationships over everything else, so I understand how friendship has gone underappreciated. Still, when I meet people who brag about not trusting anyone enough to befriend them or living and dying alone, or those who just haven't prioritized being someone's homie, it's a huge red flag for me. All it tells me is that you lack certain social skills, especially around showing up as your full self without being asked to.

When I was in middle school and high school, a lot of my female friends and I thought it was "cool" to brag about all of the guy friends we had. We spewed this bullshit proudly, with our chests, and backed it up with a pack of lies: *Girls come with too much drama. Females are just too jealous and messy. Guys aren't as superficial and gossipy—they're not always in your business. Boys are more loyal, and you can trust them more than girls.* Even if we had homegirls, we'd paint our female friendships as exceptions to our general rule of *not hanging with "females,"* a word I would never use to reference women today. I'm truly embarrassed just thinking about it, knowing what I know now. The truth is that niggas ain't shit in relationships and dating (see previous chapter), and they're not much better in friendships.

Today, I can disprove every last one of those lies we told ourselves as kids. Let a man loose in Best Buy, GameStop, or Foot Locker and see how not materialistic he is. Better yet, stand him next to another man with more money than him and see how quickly he starts trying to overcompensate. Men gossip just as much as women do, if not more, and usually about women. When men rush under women, like Ari Fletcher's Instagram posts to call her a hoe because she has a new boyfriend, that's gossiping. When they sit up in the barbershop comparing notes on a woman they both fucked, that's gossiping too. Male gossip is more acceptable because masculine communication is valued in our culture, especially when it's coated with a little misogyny. Yes, a few of my male friends have expressed their intent to not get into my business . . . but it was always when another man was making me feel uncomfortable or upset. Niggas feel no way about commenting on a woman's full sexual history, but they mind their business when their homeboys mistreat and beat up their girlfriends. Not being "messy" is the justification men use for not calling out their homies, or knocking them the fuck out, for being abusers and predators.

Very few things are more important to men than their own version of masculinity, and it shows in how they relate to the rest of the world. Collectively, straight men still haven't even figured out how to express their emotions and feel comfortable in their masculinity. Only recently have they figured out how to congratulate or comfort one another without offering some sort of "no homo" disclaimer. Most of the time they just use Black women as vehicles and outlets for their more complicated emotions. The fact that my homegirls and I ever played ourselves into thinking that men are somehow the GOAT at friendship is unfortunate, to put it kindly. So if you're a Black woman without homegirls, I'm looking at you especially sideways because not only are you lacking social skills; you've also probably pledged allegiance to the patriarchy in ways I can't get down with.

point 'em out, knock 'em out:

Here are the rules of this cruel game that my friends and I would play: We would see a stranger, point them out to someone else in our crew, and they had to go try to knock the stranger out. In best-case scenarios, the stranger would peep what we were up to and run away before we could catch them.

My decision to write about friendship after covering so many other topics was intentional. The bonds I've built with other women punctuate everything else about my life. Most of what I've learned about myself, about Black women, about trap girls, and about feminism was taught to me, in one way or another, by my friends. My homegirls have saved my life, over and over again. If you have close homegirls, you know exactly what I mean.

No one has gassed me up quite like my friends have when the rest of the world was committed to body-shaming me. We've hit so many licks and done so much illegal shit together, from recklessly playing "Point 'em out, knock 'em out" when I was a shorty to actually tussling together with grown ass men. It was my best friend who called me out and said I didn't seem happy when I embarked on my confidence journey in my twenties. My friends put me on game about money after I got tired of watching them go on trips without me when we were in college. Every step of my sexual journey in my preteen and teen years involved diligently sharing notes and resources with my friends who were on the same shit. Technically, my first abortion fundraiser happened in high school when one of my friends got pregnant. I learned how to take care of an infant when another homegirl gave birth to my first godchild not long after. Hardly any of my friends are straight, thank God, and this made stepping away from heterosexuality so much easier for me. I've already explained how my career as a sex worker began and sustained because of the friendships

I had with other women in the biz. Watching my homegirls go through similar experiences of violence and trauma is how I really grasped the different levels to which niggas ain't shit, and why I know it's not a matter of a few bad apples. In almost every other arena, my existence as a Black girl requires some sort of performance. I am my absolute truest self when I am with my homegirls, for better and for worse.

* * *

For all the ignorance I embodied when I thought having male friends was better than having female ones, I'm proud to say that I've never claimed any of my partners as my "best friend." I already have best friends, four of them, and I've never fucked any of them. It's important that I make that clear because some of y'all throw the "friend" word around all loosey-goosey to describe people you've fucked before. In the spirit of transparency, though, my closest homegirls and I have definitely run some trains before. But that is not at all the same thing as fucking my friends. There are some who would disagree, insisting that three people constitutes a threesome, but I think the line between trains and threesomes is often demarcated by friendship. (Feel free to quote me on that.) Threesomes involve three people who all want to fuck each other. Trains involve two or more people who think it would be fun to fuck the same person, together, but not each other. It's a train because the sexual energy is traveling in limited directions. I've participated in both and can definitely understand the difference. The few threesomes I've had were intimate and sexy, and (with the exception of one) did not involve anyone I considered to be a friend. The trains I've run haven't been nearly as intimate, but dammit they were fun. They were great bonding experiences for my homegirls and me. We still laugh about them to this day, but none of us are masturbating to those memories. It only ever got complicated once, when one of my homegirls caught feelings for Baller.

Lisa was actually one of my newer friends. Most of my friends go back to my elementary, middle, or high school years, but she and I met in college. We had a bunch of mutual friends, but we naturally gravitated toward each other and became inseparable. We both had a knack for hood niggas, hitting licks, cupcakes, weed, and skipping class. We were literally partners in crime. One time she was dating a drug dealer who kicked her out of the car and left her stranded at a gas station in the middle of winter. Me and my homegirl Alyn picked her up, drove straight to his house, and sent that bitch up (that's the Chicago slang equivalent to letting all hell break loose). I hit him in the jaw, Alyn had an actual pot in her back pocket that came flying out, and at some point Lisa knocked on the floor all of the product he had been bagging before we arrived. We didn't leave until he pulled his gun on us, but he definitely got the message. That's the kind of friendship we had. We were riders.

One thing about Lisa, though, was that she kept a man. She wasn't the only one of my homegirls who had a man, but her man was always the most present. She was either in between boyfriends or on a break from one of them when I introduced her to Baller. By "introduced," I mean she was invited to run the train. It went great. Per usual, we had fun. When Baller wanted her number after, I gave it to him. He was what you call "community dick," and I was under the assumption we were all on the same page about that. When Lisa mentioned that she actually liked him and wanted to date him, I laughed it off and told her I didn't mind. Looking back, I actually had a very hoity-toity attitude about the whole thing. *If she wants to fall in love with the dick man, that's on her.* Had I taken Lisa a little more seriously, I would have made the proactive decision to stop fucking Baller right then and there. But ego is a hell of a drug, and it played a big part in completely shattering our friendship.

This was new territory, but Lisa and I kept moving forward like it was normal. We still "hung out" with Baller together and separately. He and I had been fucking for years at this point, and Lisa didn't care—at least that's what she said. In retrospect, she was probably feeling just as smug as I was when I offered my blessing. *You can keep sucking his dick all you want, but he has feelings for me.* Baller and I had never been in love or super affectionate. But before this new arrangement, I saw him as my equal, and vice versa. Now his and Lisa's new energy made me feel like an underling in some emotional hierarchy I was expected to accept. I felt some type of way when we'd walk into his place and Lisa would get a passionate kiss while I'd get a cute hug and blunt rolled for the occasion. But because I'd given my blessing, I couldn't articulate my discomfort. Lisa was starting to feel some type of way that I was still fucking her new boo and that because he and I had known each other for so long there were things I knew about him and his personality that she didn't. But because she'd given her blessing, she couldn't articulate her feelings either. Neither of us wanted to admit that we'd changed our minds, so we doubled down.

Suddenly we were in a battle of wills and egos, and as we kept moving forward like nothing had changed, every little thing started to feel like a jab. We eventually started to talk about it, endlessly, and often with our mutual best friend having to listen to both sides over and over again. But rather than getting to the heart of our issues, we were just making cases for how neither of us had done anything wrong. Rather than helping, many of these conversations only served to further erode our trust in each other and build up our resentments. Our friendship was literally deteriorating before our eyes. I didn't want to be the girl who lost one of her best friends over some dick. So rather than try to dissect our respective relationships with Baller, I implored Lisa to consider: *What about us?*

She wasn't receptive to that, at all. She didn't think she should have to give up the new guy in her life who was making her happy. I'd given my blessing, they'd caught feelings, and now it was out of everyone's hands. The way she saw it was that if my happiness was contingent on her and Baller falling back, then I was no friend to her at all. During one of our particularly heated conversations, in which I was once again wondering, *What about us?* she looked me dead in the eye and said: "I'm not fucking you." In other words, the "us" she was prioritizing was her and Baller. This was a breaking point for me. I felt betrayed, abandoned, and, for the first time since everything had started, truly heartbroken. This was the day our friendship, as both of us knew it, ended.

I've been through breakups and loss, but when Lisa and I broke up, it was by far one of the most difficult things I've ever had to endure. It took Lisa only a couple of months to realize that Baller wasn't shit. He was living out of a backpack and still had feelings for his ex when they stopped dating. But it took years for her and I to rebuild a bond that was anything close to what we'd had before she met him. We could never avoid each other because we have too many shared homegirls. But for so long it was painful to be around each other because we were both still hurting from what had happened. Much like when the tensions were first building between us, we tried to talk it out a few times. Once again we avoided the real issues, and our reconciliation felt like an endless process that wasn't going anywhere. We were cordial and friendly, but everything had changed between us. Neither of us was asking for forgiveness. We just saw each other in a completely new way, and neither of us was sure that we liked what we saw.

Deep down inside us both, though, was that bond we'd built as friends. Real friends. We still loved each other. Plus, we had a community of homegirls around us who loved us too. They kept Lisa and I on a path back to each other. To this day, Lisa credits all of us, her homegirls, with teaching her how to be a better person and a friend. She was very accustomed to being the responsible daughter, the reliable sister, the dependable aunt, and the supportive girlfriend. Friendship often took a back seat in her life. She understood how hurt I was by her words and her choices once she realized how much having homegirls meant to her. Meanwhile, I had to acknowledge that I had been hiding behind my friendships and not actually showing up in them how I was supposed to. I loved my friends, but I loved *having* friends more. I lived vicariously through them. I used them as deflectors to avoid confronting the shit I needed to deal with within myself.

For years I'd questioned Lisa's loyalty to me because I wanted her to think about romantic relationships the exact same way I did. The only perspective I was willing to consider was that Lisa was okay with throwing our friendship away for the sake of her relationship. When, in reality, I was too willing to throw our friendship away just because she's a "relationship girl" and I'm not. I had to remind myself that I don't get to dictate my friend's feelings. I don't get to dispose of them when they make choices I wouldn't make. To be a real friend, I have to honor my homegirls' boundaries, even if I don't share them. I have to respect their perspectives, even when they might be inconvenient to my ego. I should actually pay especially close attention when I feel my ego is in danger. (That kind of self-awareness could have spared me from a few more years of fucking Baller, to be honest.) I had to accept Lisa for who she was. But more important, I had to have empathy for her. That's how we were able to reconnect on the other side of so much strife. That's why I'm still her rider and why I'd still run up in a trap nigga's house for her, to this day.

* * *

I'm proud to say that I got the homegirl gene honest. I got it from my mama. The first dwellings I have memories in aren't ones my mama was on the lease for. Rather, I remember us living with her friends when we were in between cribs or on hard times. My grandparents kicked my mama out shortly after she had my sister as a teenager. Without the support of her family, she turned to friends to keep her afloat. One of those friends introduced her to my dad, and later let us stay with her when my daddy (may he rest in peace) wasn't financially stable enough to keep a roof over our heads. My mama has always kept a few homegirls, some of whom she's had since before I was born. She's been able to rely on them, consistently, to make sure that both she and I were taken care of when she was struggling or in times of transition. I've also watched her return the favor now that she's older, a homeowner, and more financially stable.

When I say my homegirls have saved my life, I truly mean it. Homegirls have been the difference between me having a roof over my head and being on the streets. They've kept me out of jail. They've loaned and gifted me money so I could have basic necessities when I needed them. It's been established that historically we cannot rely on these niggas. As such, Black women have been the biggest advocates for Black women. We're our biggest protectors. We're our riders. Over and over again we've proven that we're the only ones who got us. I lean in to friendship so hard because if we are going to survive this shit, we actually *need* each other. I think my mama understands this too, which is probably why she's so supportive of my friendships. She knows they could very likely be the difference between my life and death. I'm glad she's gotten to witness my friendships grow and evolve over the years.

I started building my little network of friends—all of their names have been changed—from the moment I was school age. I met three of my four best friends, Nola, Tasha, and Nicolette, before I was even in middle school. Lisa is the fourth. I spent so much time at Jasmine's house in middle school and high school that she's more like my sister, and Dakita was our sneaky ass cousin. But since then, I've made even more. I didn't meet Simone—whom I lovingly refer to as my "wife" because we bicker about dumb shit like what to watch on TV—until I was in graduate school. Keeping up with my friends as they've spread all around the country and the world hasn't been nearly as easy.

I came up with a solution in 2015 when I invited my homegirls to a secluded lake house in Georgia to catch up. The seclusion was important because I wanted time for us to just sit in one another's faces and talk. There would be no makeup, going out, or dealing with the world. It was just for us. I got to introduce friends from different parts of my life to each other. We cooked and cleaned together. We talked and laughed and danced and drank and ate and got high as hell together. I called it "homegirl retreat," and I decided to do it every year. So far I've done four of them, and will continue to do them. They're a consistent highlight of my year, where I know I can recharge. I'm currently in the process of creating a blueprint for other Black women to have their own homegirl retreats.

I've spent a lot of time in this book defining a trap feminist framework that is self-reflective and individualistic. It calls on Black women to be aggressively self-interested as a means of self-determination. Trap feminism is not a formal political policy for ending our oppression, and that's by design. (A wise man once said, "Ain't got on no suits cuz we ain't tryna be presidents."[2]) Trap feminism merely questions how Black women and femmes have been left ass out by not prioritizing ourselves. Still, it's hard to divest from the specific kind of misogynoir that continues to disrupt and endanger the life of Black women without losing our own humanity in the process. That's why friendship is so important. It keeps our loyalty, ethics, empathy, and morality in check. Friendship keeps us humble and reminds us to be good to people while supporting our greatest strengths.

I'm seeing this in female rap too. For all the scamming and not calling back that City Girls do to men, their love for one another in sisterhood is the most tender part of their personas.

Megan Thee Stallion made an intentional decision to include her real friends from Texas in her music videos, her social media, and her schedule as she was breaking onto the scene. When Cardi B dropped the visuals for her "WAP" video and included other rappers like Mulatto, Rubi Rose, and Sukihana, then did an interview with all of them right after, I felt a serious change in the tide. Not only do we have more women than ever to choose from and listen to, they also are linking with each other and becoming friends because they know there is power in those connections. If there is any hope for Black women, in the music industry or anywhere else, it's because other Black women are here to hold us down.

REAL BITCH

Real bitch. Authentic. Best believe I put my heart in it.

—Chella H with Sasha Go Hard, "Real Bitch"[1]

When I was shopping around the proposal for this book, one of the editors who passed on it offered my agent some feedback. Publishers like to keep the target audience for their books pretty broad, and this editor, a Black woman, thought that focusing on the specific subset of trap girls left way too many folks out. Her feedback was that women who were older, more settled into professional lives, or even those who didn't have ties to the hood wouldn't be able to relate. For her, trap feminism felt like something that only young, ratchet Black girls could relate to.

It was a disappointing take on my work but one that made sense in the context of our current landscape. We're obsessed with Black women right now. Names like Tracee Ellis Ross and Elaine Welteroth are trendy and zeitgeisty as Black women who represent affluence, success, and taste making. They're amazing women, but their proximity to institutions and industries of power have made them more marketable and easier

ratchet:

Reclaimed and embraced by some Black women
to simply mean lively and exciting, "ratchet"
is often used to describe Black women who
are considered ghetto and uncouth.

to love. Within the media industry, many of my colleagues who are tapped to weigh in on Black culture are those with similar access and backgrounds. They come from privilege I did not know and they have had to untangle their Blackness from the web of whiteness they were socialized in. We're obsessed with Black girls who have reached these heights of assimilation. Seriously, if I have to see another fucking series, movie, article, podcast, or stage play about a Black girl self-actualizing in her mostly white school, friend group, neighborhood, relationship, or job, I am going to scream.

I get why so much room has been carved out for these kinds of Black girls. Reckoning with whiteness and expectations of the white gaze is a valid part of the Black experience, especially in the US. But these Black women do represent the majority of us. Most of us learned to love our hair, our bodies, our skin, our people, and our culture by just having them. I would actually question if we had to "learn" how to do those things at all. For most Black girls, it was just part of our upbringing to rock with ourselves and our culture.

It's the same culture that inspires trap music. Have most Black women lived in housing projects or ghettos, sold pussy, been arrested, and gotten into at least one physical fight in their lifetimes? No. But are most Black women touched by the realities of economic uncertainty, hair discrimination, intimate-partner violence, bias, sexual repression, and/or hosting other intersecting oppressions at some point in their lives? You're damn right. As such, we've all benefited from the resourceful and creative responses to the disenfranchisement I've outlined in this book—the responses that were innovated by the ratchet Black girls. Even if it's something as simple as laying our baby hair down or always knowing how to find the best deal on school clothes.

Even an artsy chick who's into crystals and meditation can like to shake her ass. Fat body-positive influencers are using female rap to frame their ideologies around radical self-love. Even though they don't inhabit bodies that look like the women in the music industry, they've rallied around the idea that their marginalized bodies also deserve luxury. I've been to events attended by alums of Ivy Leagues and employees of Big Pharma who are Black. Their degrees and prestigious STEM jobs aside, they also like trap music and my long ass nails.

People try to erase ratchet Black girls at every turn, but we are not siloed, and our impact is undeniable. In the same way that hip-hop is consumed by diverse audiences all over the world, so are the trends that are set by ghetto ass Black girls. Our style, our language, and our beauty resonate with people across different backgrounds. Just look at all the white influencers who are making millions by appropriating Black culture or flat-out "Blackfishing." Everyone wants a fat ass and a colorful weave. It's not a coincidence that the editor who ended up being the most excited about the potential of this book is a white woman (God bless you, Hilary). People are obsessed with hood bitches, whether we care to admit it or not.

But to the point of that first editor who passed on my proposal, there are some things about trap feminism that cannot be contained by theory, politics, or curriculum. It's about the values you were raised with and the conditioning you were socialized under. And that *is* hard to translate to a "broader audience." A lot of trap feminism is about having "heart." It's a unique cocktail of integrity, common sense, confidence, empathy, courage, and resilience. These are traits you can't quantify or learn out of a textbook. If you've made it this far and you're still wondering whether or not you're a trap feminist, you need to ask yourself something that you've probably never been asked on a job interview or even a date. Are you a *real* bitch? Being a real bitch is fundamentally more important than being a bad bitch, a rich bitch, a freak bitch, or even *that* bitch, because all of those things are dictated to us by a culture that relies on our subjugation.

Can you make good judgment calls under pressure? Do you say what you mean and mean what you say? Are you principled when it comes to your people? This is the real spirit of trap feminism. I don't think this shit is new either. I like to think that Harriet Tubman was a trap feminist. Trap feminism was in Joan Morgan's *When Chickenheads Come Home to Roost* and on Lil' Kim's *Hard Core* album. Now it's found in Mulatto's debut album, *Queen of Da Souf,* and named explicitly in this book. In ten years it may have transformed into something else as Black girls continue to traverse the physical and digital worlds and engage with new forms of technology and adversity.

When I envision a trap feminist future, it's one in which even more Black women are willing to lead with the intention to be real bitches. There is hope for me in that future. It's a future that allows for Black women to be our full selves without fear of mockery, denial, judgment, persecution, violence, or death. We can build relationships and families that fit the needs of our lives, as opposed to socially acceptable scripted versions that require us to sacrifice parts of ourselves. I'm looking forward to a future in which we can love who we want, fuck who we want, and turn up how we want. We can stay in our bags and actually enjoy the fruits of our labor, without having to sacrifice any parts of who we are in order to get there. We'll be able to stand in all that power, smacking our lips, rolling our necks, playing our games, and singing our songs.

I wanted to write this book because the stories of Black girls like Nina Pop and Breonna Taylor should be included in the Black cultural lexicon *before* it's time to put their faces on a T-shirt. It's cute to call out non-Black folks for cultural appropriation while judging Black women with thick, fake lash extensions and outfits from Rainbow for not making their style choices more *Vogue* adjacent. I wrote this book because ghetto girls are more than political martyrs and mood boards. We are not caricatures, and we don't need to be saved. We deserve to be heard, have our humanity taken seriously, and trusted to lead our own rebellions and revolutions. Until then, we'll keep whippin' in our kitchens, finessing, and glowing up the best ways we know how.

ACKNOWLEDGMENTS

I have to acknowledge the women of family, my foundation, first. Tete, thank you for introducing me to beauty, self-care, and indulgence before anyone else. We all need more of it in our lives. You deserve all the happiness and peace in the world, and a vacation. Dana, my sister, you were the first baddie I knew. I will never forget how stunning you were with your '90s updo and your hands, neck, and ears dripped in gold. You were my first idol. Granny, thank you for holding this family down. You are the soil from which we all grew to new heights. Your love and your prayers are the reason I am still here. Ma, you are the most resilient person I know. I got some of my best qualities, like my love for reading and my smart mouth, from you. I'm proud of that, I am proud of you, and I am proud of us for making it this far. Jayna, one day you might read this and understand why you inspire me so much with your curiosity and empathy. For all the ways that we are different, we are the same and I love all of you so much.

To my homegirls, I don't even know where to begin. I wouldn't be who I am without y'all. To Kristen, Porshe, Aerian, Charne, Stacy, Tova, and Lisa, thank you for the laughs and the unconditional support. Niqua, my first real best friend, thank you for being the blueprint. We've been picking up where we left off for almost twenty-five years. To Whitney and Timesha, some of the happiest moments of my life were the ones we had together. Damillia and Danielle, I will never doubt the power of fresh starts and new beginnings thanks to you two. Thank you for giving me a chance to get it right. Donna, thank you for being my sister in the trenches. Nikita, your trust in me makes me want to be a better person. Tell Avi I love her. Treasure, Cherea, and Gabby, here's to another twenty years. Jocindeé, you are more amazing than you even know. To Amber, Chelsea S., Shonda, and my wife Layci, thank you for reminding me that I am never too old to make new friends. To my Unbothered homegirls: thank you for growing from work friends to real friends. Boochie, thank you for being one of my greatest loves. Everyone deserves a you. There are a bunch more of you that I could name. Y'all know exactly who you are. Every word of encouragement got me here.

This book, or trap feminism, would not exist without my fairy god-homegirl, Dr. Ruth Nicole Brown, her brilliant work on Black Girlhood, and her commitment to celebrating us. Rest assured that SOLHOT did exactly what it was supposed to do. I also want to give a special shout-out to my lil homies, my daughters, Talisha, Chelsea M., and Taylor. Keep making me proud. To that end, I must also shout out Joan Morgan for the foundation she laid with hip-hop feminism.

To the love of my life, my Genius Bae. I wrote 90 percent of this book in the comfort of your apartment. I wrote all of it basking in the comfort of your love. Thank you for being a true partner to me, for giving me space and cheering me on whenever I needed it. I love you.

Speaking of writing spaces, I have to thank DJ Raphael. We've never met, but the only things I listened to while writing this book were your YouTube mixes. Thank you for your ear and for the vibes. (Shout-out to my homegirl Kris for putting me on.)

Thank you to my literary agent, Nicki Richesin, for getting this off the ground. Thank you Gabrielle Korn, for, among other things, sharing your lit agent with me. Hilary Swanson, thank you and your team for going so hard for this book and believing in what I had to say.

Last but not least, I want to thank the rap girls for providing the soundtrack to my life and inspiring me to be a bad bitch, and, more important, a real one.

NOTES

INTRODUCTION: TRAP FEMINISM

1. Yo Gotti and Zed Zilla, "I Wanna Fuck," track 4 on *Cocaine Muzik 4: Gangsta Grillz*, I & E, 2015, compact disc.
2. Travis Porter, "Make It Rain," track 12 on *From Day 1*, RCA Records, 2012, compact disc.
3. Trick Daddy and Trina, "Nann Nigga," track 6 on www.thug.com, Slip-N-Slide Records, 1998, compact disc.
4. Megan Thee Stallion, "Big Ole Freak," track 7 on *Tina Snow*, 1501 Certified Ent. LLC, 2018, digital.
5. Gucci Mane and DG Yola, "Im a Dog," track 25 on *The State vs. Radric Davis (Deluxe)*, Warner Records, 2009, compact disc.

CHAPTER 1: BAD BITCHES ONLY

1. Gucci Mane and Kanye West, "Pussy Print," track 5 on *Everybody Looking*, Atlantic Recording Corporation, 2016, compact disc.
2. Young Dolph, "Get Paid," track 8 on *King of Memphis*, Paper Route Empire, 2016, compact disc.
3. DJ Khaled and Drake, "For Free," single, We The Best/Epic Records, 2016, digital.
4. bell hooks, *Writing Beyond Race: Living Theory and Practice* (New York: Routledge, 2013), 4.
5. Megan Thee Stallion, "WTF I Want," track 1 on *Tina Snow*, 1501 Certified Ent. LLC, 2018, digital.
6. Plies, "Ran Off on Da Plug Twice," single, Slip-N-Slide Records, 2016, digital.
7. Rae Sremmurd, "No Type," track 10 on *SremmLife*, Eardruma/Interscope Records, 2014, compact disc.

CHAPTER 2: KNUCKIN', BUCKIN', READY TO FIGHT

1. Crime Mob and Lil Scrappy, "Knuck If You Buck," track 2 on *Crime Mob*, Reprise Records, 2004, compact disc.
2. City Girls, "Act Up," track 2 on *Girl Code*, Quality Control LLC, 2019, digital.
3. Nicki Minaj, "Episode 8," Queen Radio, Apple Music 1, September 10, 2018, digital.
4. LaMonda Stallings, "Hip Hop and the Black Ratchet Imagination," *Palimpsest* 2, no. 2 (2013): 135–139.

5. Audre Lorde, "The Uses of Anger," *Sister Outsider: Essays and Speeches* (Trumansburg, NY: Crossings, 1984), 124.
6. Laurel Thatcher Ulrich, *Well-Behaved Women Seldom Make History* (New York: Alfred A. Knopf, 2007).

CHAPTER 3: FIVE-STAR BITCH

1. Megan Thee Stallion, "Savage," track 2 on *Suga*, 1501 Certified Ent. LLC, 2020, digital.

CHAPTER 4: RUN ME MY MONEY

1. Megan Thee Stallion and Beyoncé, "Savage (Remix)," track 15 on *Good News*, 1501 Certified Ent. LLC, 2020, digital.

CHAPTER 5: PLAN B

1. Sukihana, "Cardi B: The WAP Interview," New Music Daily Radio, Apple Music 1, August 7, 2020, digital.

CHAPTER 6: SELLING IT

1. UGK and Outkast, "Int'l Players Anthem (I Choose You)," track 2 on *UGK (Underground Kingz)*, Zomba Recording LLC, 2006, compact disc.

CHAPTER 7: NOT STRAIGHT

1. Dream Doll and Fivio Foreign, "Ah Ah Ah," single, District 18, 2020, digital.
2. LaMonda Stallings, "Hip Hop and the Black Ratchet Imagination," *Palimpsest* 2, no. 2 (2013): 135–139.

CHAPTER 8: FUCK THESE NIGGAS

1. Saucy Santana and Tokyo Jetz, "Boy Damn," track 9 on *Pretty Little Gangsta*, Arena Music Productions LLC, 2020, digital.
2. Blackburn Center, "Black Women & Domestic Violence," accessed August 10, 2020, https://www.blackburncenter.org/post/2020/02/26/black-women -domestic-violence.

CHAPTER 9: MY BITCHES

1. Dreezy and Gucci Mane, "We Gon' Ride," track 2 on *No Hard Feelings*, Interscope Records, 2016, compact disc.
2. Lil Wayne, "Tha Block Is Hot," track 2 on *Tha Block Is Hot*, Cash Money Records, 1999, compact disc.

EPILOGUE: REAL BITCH

1. Chella H and Sasha Go Hard, "Real Bitch," on *The Morning After Pill*, RBA Records, 2013, compact disc.